Plants

for

Small

Spaces

PLANTS *for* SMALL SPACES

STEPHANIE DONALDSON
— & —
SUSAN BERRY

FIREFLY BOOKS

A Firefly Book

Published in Canada in 1998 by Firefly Books Ltd.
3680 Victoria Park Avenue, Willowdale, Ontario, Canada M2H 3K1

Canadian Cataloguing in Publication Data:

Donaldson, Stephanie
Plants for small spaces

Includes index.
ISBN 1–55209–281–X

1. Miniature plants. 2. Gardens, Miniature. 3. Container gardening.
I. Berry, Susan, 1944–   . II. Title.

SB433.5.D66 1998   635.9'67   C98–931160–0

A Berry Book, conceived, edited and designed for Collins & Brown Limited.
First published in Great Britain in 1998 by Collins & Brown Limited,
London House, Great Eastern Wharf, Parkgate Road, London SW11 4NQ.

Editor Jane Struthers
Section Editors Alison Freegard and Amanda Lebentz
Executive Editor Ginny Surtees

Designer Roger Daniels
Managing Art Editor Kevin Williams

Photography Michelle Garrett, Howard Rice and Steven Wooster

Printed and bound in Hong Kong.

Contents

INTRODUCTION

We have all used the phrase "small is beautiful" at one

time or another and this is certainly the effect we strive

for when gardening in small spaces. By using the vertical

as well as the horizontal surfaces you can greatly increase

the potential planting areas, and the addition of raised

containers will allow vertical planting away from the

boundaries. With gardening

on this scale, every inch is

precious and good seasonal

planting is needed to ensure

there is color and interest

throughout the year. Even the

tiniest space needs drama, as well as good plantings, and

the inclusion of a large pot with a striking plant, a

column, or a statue will create a focal point to complete

the design of your small, but beautiful, space.

ABOVE *Even steps can provide an ideal place for planting, as this complementary group of scented herbs, busy lizzies, chrysanthemums, and fuchsia demonstrates.*

RIGHT *Not an inch of space is lost for planting on this small terrace, with its wonderful display of summer-flowering annuals, including scented tobacco plants, petunias, and lobelia, many in raised containers.*

THE CHALLENGE OF gardening in a small space lies in using the limited area as effectively as possible to create the kind of garden that suits you and your lifestyle. All the ideas in this book are easily achievable and there is no structural work involved, beyond putting up a hook for a hanging basket, but there are lots of inspiring ideas to help you transform the garden you have into the garden you want. *Plants for Small Spaces* introduces you to a range of planting concepts that will help you get the most out of your garden by using all the surfaces available to you. Walls, windowsills, doorways, steps, corners, the terraced patio, or the balcony – all can be adorned with plants that trail, climb, or spread from pots, troughs, and hanging baskets. Container planting is an essential element of gardening in a small space, and you will find plenty of inspiration for every shape and size of container, as well as practical advice on how to be a successful container gardener.

The final section of this book, the Plant Finder, will help you to select suitable plants for the conditions in your garden, plants that will perform well throughout

ABOVE *The architectural beauty of topiary plants contrasts interestingly with the informal background.*

the year, fill your garden with color, shape, and

texture, and enable you to achieve the overall effect

you desire. The great bonus of gardening in a small

space is that it allows you time – time to experiment, to

plan, and to sit and enjoy the fruits of your labor. Don't

envy those with larger gardens – time is a luxury they

seldom enjoy.

BELOW *Shade is no obstacle to planting small spaces: busy lizzies in an antique wire container, hostas, little blue creeping campanulas, purple-leaved* Heuchera, *and a host of other foliage plants are crammed together in a richly textured tapestry.*

PLANTING CONCEPTS

Plants play many roles in the garden but in a small space the planting schemes, and combinations of plants, have to be carefully chosen so they perform to greatest effect. Background color, instant effects, seasonal variety and vertical, as well as horizontal, plantings are all ways in which to get the most from

your plants and keep your space looking colorful throughout the seasons. Also, different forms of plants can be used for different situations and surfaces.

ABOVE *Neatly clipped topiary boxwood balls provide a textural and architectural contrast with blowzy lilies. The elegant striped pots emphasize the arrangement.*

RIGHT *Formality plays an important role in small-space planting; its architectural shapes create a foil for more ephemeral seasonal flower color.*

*I*N GENERAL, THERE *are two approaches to planting. There is the rational approach, in which the gardener allows the space to dictate the planting, and the acquisitive approach, embodied by the gardener who yearns to grow a particular plant and will find a way to fit it into the available space. The rational gardener enjoys formal gardening and appreciates controlled color schemes and symmetry, while the acquisitive gardener is more at home with the informal style of garden plants where color is riotous, plants climb or sprawl, and the design evolves more by happy accident than planning. You will find gardening more fulfilling if you decide at the start which approach most appeals to you. If you long for a miniature Versailles, love topiary, and prefer single-color schemes, you are a rationalist who will enjoy planning your garden on paper and will have the patience to train plants. If, on the other hand, you love impulse buying and like to experiment, then you are an acquisitive gardener who will enjoy an informal garden. Once you have decided which category suits you, you will have some guidelines to work within. For example, vertical planting in the formal garden should be largely evergreen with flowering plants as accent color, while the informal garden benefits from a colorful succession of flowers.*

ABOVE *Handsome foliage plants make a welcome change from bright flowers, and create a useful focal point.*

FACING PAGE *Planting in tiers, using attractive terracotta and metal raised containers, makes maximum use of available space and creates the illusion of a much larger garden.*

VERTICAL PLANTING

In the short term, pots and planters may be used to decorate walls and fences in a small garden, but they are fairly labor-intensive and the better long-term solution is to plant your boundaries with a selection of climbing plants. A combination of climbers will provide year-round interest.

THERE ARE many beautiful climbers that will happily intertwine and provide a succession of glorious flowers and foliage to brighten the gloomiest corner or the dullest wall. Although most climbing plants prefer to be positioned where they enjoy some sunshine, it is surprising how many, including some varieties of roses, honeysuckle, and clematis, as well as ivy, will thrive on a shady wall (see pages 120-1).

The key to growing climbing plants successfully on walls and fences in a small garden is the careful choice of suitable varieties and good soil preparation, followed by regular fertilizing and pruning. It is possible to grow climbing plants in large containers, although they will do better and need less attention if they are planted in the ground. A surprisingly small area is needed: for example, a bed of just 1 × 2ft (30 × 60cm) was needed for the honeysuckle (*Lonicera*) and potato vine (*Solanum crispum* 'Glasnevin') in the main picture. This same bed also contained a climbing rose, which had flowered earlier in the season, along with an underplanting of lilies and rosemary.

TOP *Clematis 'The Vagabond' twines with a star jasmine (Trachelospermum diffusum).*

ABOVE *Boston ivy (Parthenocissus tricuspidata) or Virginia creeper (P. quinquefolia) will rapidly cover a brick wall, without the need for any supporting structure. It makes an ideal backdrop for more colorful displays in containers.*

LEFT *A black-painted fence with horizontal wire supports is the backdrop for a lush summer display of pink 'New Dawn' roses and mauve clematis 'Prince Charles.'*

FACING PAGE *This planting of honeysuckle and potato vine in contrasting yellows and purples ensures a long-lasting display.*

FOCAL POINTS

Whether you know it or not, your garden already has a focal point – the point to which the eye naturally travels when entering or viewing the garden. If you are lucky, this will be something attractive – possibly a tree, an architectural plant, or a statue. Yet, unattractive features can draw the eye just as powerfully and may need to be removed, disguised, or supplanted by a different, more attractive focal point before the full potential of the garden can be realized.

DEPENDING ON the size and shape of your garden, you may have more than one focal point. Generally speaking, any clearly defined area should have a single focal point and this is determined by looking at the area from the most used viewpoint – attempting to create other focal points from different viewpoints can result in a rather muddled, overdone, effect. It doesn't matter that viewing the focal point from different aspects may not reveal it in its full glory; this adds an element of mystery to the garden and encourages the observer to explore it even more. Some of the most successful gardens rely on this type of effect.

If the view beyond your boundaries is worth looking at, you can add distance and perspective to your focal point by raising it and framing it against a backdrop of the view beyond. For example, you can place a statue or urn on a plinth rather than leave it at ground level. This immediately gives the object increased visual importance. Alternatively, you can plant a group of taller, flowering

shrubs behind the statue or urn to draw the eye up. Conversely, if the view over the fence leaves a lot to be desired, then the focal point should be at a low level to encourage the eye away from the offending blot on the landscape. A pond or other water feature is particularly effective, especially if it includes some

running water, which is usually an irresistible draw. This adds another dimension to your garden and creates a very tranquil effect that is particularly refreshing in the hot summer months.

In many small spaces, one of the most important functions of a focal point is to add height to what can sometimes be a rather flat plane. This can be done by creating a point of interest on a wall, by playing with scale, and including a large architectural feature, or through the use of topiary. At nighttime, some well positioned lighting will add extra drama to the scene.

In a garden with no obvious focal point you can locate the most effective position by placing a fairly tall object, such as a stepladder, at various points around the garden until you find the position that has the most interesting effect on the shape and perspective of the garden. This will be your focal point.

LEFT This statue of a young girl draws the eye through the layers of plants in a mixed herbaceous border. She is surrounded by phlox and balsam (Impatiens balsamina) flowers.

BELOW Even a hedge can form a backdrop to a focal point. Here, an alcove has been cut in the hedge to provide a home for a stone bust. This creates a sense of mystery and surprise for the visitor who may not notice the statue at first. In the winter, when the herbaceous border dies back, the stone bust will be revealed in all its splendor.

LEFT A shady bower has been created from trellis, which allows you to see into the garden beyond while creating a backdrop to the ornate metal seating. The bower is completed by the stone mask, which hangs from the top of the trellis.

RIGHT The base of a tree forms the focal point for a statue and a mixed summer planting of petunias, marguerites, agapanthus, and helichrysum. All these plants are in containers that can be removed when the flowering display is over; this way, you can create different plantings for each season.

WIGWAM FOR CLIMBERS

Tall-growing, colorful plants are an important element in a small garden because they provide height. Wall plants such as roses (Rosa), clematis (Clematis), and honeysuckle (Lonicera) will form the backdrop, but you can enjoy wonderful additional color with climbing annuals, such as sweet peas (Lathyrus odoratus), nasturtiums (Tropaeolum), morning glories (Ipomoea), and even runner beans (Phaseolus), planted in large pots and encouraged to climb twiggy sticks.

ALTHOUGH sweet peas (*Lathyrus odoratus*) are sometimes available at florists in summer as cut flowers, it is rare for them to be as richly scented as the garden-grown varieties. Growing a pot of sweet peas will provide a double pleasure – fragrance and color in the garden and a prolific supply of cut flowers throughout the summer months.

Traditionally, sweet peas were grown in straight rows in very fertile soil in the kitchen garden. Side-shoots were ruthlessly pinched out and only the finest, straightest-stalked blooms were allowed to reach maturity. Plant breeders concentrated on developing large blooms at the cost of fragrance and there was eventually a danger that these lovely flowers would become insipid, overblown shadows of their glorious ancestors. Fortunately, there is a real revival of interest in the old varieties and it is once again easy to buy sweet pea seeds or young plants in which color and fragrance are equally important.

Sweet peas grow surprisingly well in large pots provided that they are planted in good potting soil enriched with composted humus. A regular liquid fertilizer will ensure a long flowering period, which will also be encouraged by picking the flowers as soon as they have opened. If flowers are left to set seed on the plants, the flowering season will be much shorter.

Most annual climbers need similar treatment, although nasturtiums are the exception. They do better in poor soil.

HOW TO GROW SWEET PEAS IN A POT

You can use ordinary 5ft (1.5m) garden canes to support sweet peas grown in a pot, but twiggy sticks will look more decorative and the sweet peas will be able to climb through them without the aid of plant rings. A 16in (40cm) pot is roomy enough for 10-12 plants spaced evenly around the edge of the pot. Sweet peas grow well from seed. The seeds are large and easy to handle. Plant them in a 6in (15cm) diameter pot about $1/2$in (1cm) deep and $1/2$in (1cm) apart. Put the pot in good light and keep moist. When they are about 3in (8cm) tall, they can be transplanted to the larger pot and supported with canes or sticks.

1 *Take a large pot and cover the base with broken shards of pot to create a drainage layer before partially filling with potting soil.*

2 *Fill the pot with a mixture of potting soil and composted humus. Plant the sweet pea seedlings around the pot edge.*

3 *Firmly push the twigs or canes into position between the evenly spaced sweet pea plants.*

4 *Tie the twigs or canes together to form a wigwam. Canes will only need tying at the top, whereas twigs may need more restraint.*

LEFT *Be sure to position your sweet peas where you can best enjoy their beauty and fragrance. A sunny, sheltered corner where you like to sit is ideal, or next to a path or French windows where the scent will stop you in your tracks.*

ABOVE *Picking sweet peas encourages the plants to keep flowering. At the height of the summer you will be able to pick flowers every day, although as the season progresses, the stems will get shorter and shorter.*

SEASONAL DISPLAYS

Gardening in small spaces is at its best when there is a succession of plantings throughout the year. These do not need to be elaborate or expensive – two or three containers filled with plants in their prime are all that is needed to transform a rather gloomy winter garden. Similarly, a group of pots planted with miniature bulbs placed on a wall or table will entice you out into the early spring sunshine to admire their beauty and fragrance.

THE GARDEN, patio, or balcony can, if you choose, undergo a transformation each season. Although impulse buying when plants are flowering is not generally recommended during the summer when the result is often very short-lived plants, buying plants this way during the cooler months allows you to assemble instant displays that will last well.

At the same time, a little planning can ensure color throughout the year. Bulbs planted under herbaceous plants in the fall will provide fresh color in the spring when the herbaceous plants are starting to send out green shoots. During the summer and fall months, colorful annuals and half-hardy perennials will provide strong color in containers and fill any gaps in the borders. Evergreen and fruiting or berried shrubs and climbers will give color and structure to the garden throughout the fall and winter.

You can have some containers that you earmark for changing displays, replanting them each season. This is almost always the case with window-boxes, since if this is your entire gardening space, you cannot simply move the containers to a more out of the way spot when the plants are past their best. Such a scheme could involve cyclamens, heathers, and winter-flowering pansies

in the colder months; small scillas, primulas, and dwarf narcissi in the spring; verbena or helichrysum with trailing diascias and geraniums in the summer; and chrysanthemums with pernettya and small foliage plants in fall. With a terraced patio or small backyard at your disposal, you can have more permanent seasonal displays, simply moving containers into the foreground or background, as the state of their planting dictates.

LEFT AND ABOVE *Troughs and smaller containers filled with tulips and other spring flowers add instant color to a dark corner in the garden.*

TOP, ABOVE, AND RIGHT *Hanging baskets, windowboxes, and other containers do not have to look subdued in the winter months. A windowbox of purple ornamental cabbages and pink heathers (top) makes a vivid splash of color in fall, while a hanging basket of mixed pansies and primulas (above and right) looks cheerful in early spring.*

INSTANT EFFECTS

Although long-term planning is generally advised in gardening, there are times when you simply can't wait. Maybe the garden needs transforming for a special party, the summer border flowered early in the season and is now lacking color, or a house move means you have inherited a rather dull garden which needs brightening up while you make long-term plans. Whatever the reason, planted containers can create an instant change of scene.

For a small garden to look its best consistently, you need to emphasize the plants that are looking good and disguise those that aren't. This can be done with groupings of container plants set against a backdrop of structural plants growing in borders and up walls and fences. You can then bring plants to the front as they come into flower and tuck those that are past their best into the background. Planted in containers of different sizes and heights, a group of herbaceous plants can create an instant summer border, and when underplanted with bulbs they also provide spring color. Many evergreens grow happily in pots and can be used to provide year-round color even when not in flower. Evergreen variegated plants are very useful because they can add depth and interest to a group of plants that might otherwise look rather dull. With a core collection of shrubs and perennials you can then add color with annuals and half-hardy perennials.

Moving large containers can be heavy work, so choose a fairly permanent position for these and only move them when a complete change of scene is needed. However, you should get into the habit of moving the smaller containers around frequently. You don't need to move them all, just two or three at a time will create a constantly changing view.

Be bold for that special occasion. Get help and move all the containers around to give a change of focus, then spend some time tidying, weeding, and trimming so that each plant looks its best. Choose a color scheme and go for it in a big way using blocks of color – two or three containers densely planted with a single color will make much more impact than a mixed planting.

LEFT AND ABOVE *At first glance, the border (left) appears to be a richly planted herbaceous bed in its full summer glory. Tobacco plants, helichrysum, Lysimachia, rosemary, and penstemon are all flowering their hearts out while a golden hop clambers up a trellis. The photograph above reveals the truth – the plants are in carefully arranged containers while foliage hides the pots and creates the impression of a planted border.*

RIGHT AND FAR RIGHT *You can buy flowering plants and bulbs from a garden center and create instant displays in the early spring. This tub has been planted with daffodils, white Dicentra, and hyacinths.*

FORMS OF CONTAINER

When gardening in a small space, the container is king – it gives the garden flexibility and allows for transformations that would not be possible if all planting was in the soil. Each container is in effect a miniature garden with its own soil conditions, climate, and aspect, all of which you can control.

Whether positioned singly or grouped to create layers of plantings, containers make up the furniture of the garden, without which the space can look bare and incomplete.

ABOVE *Chrysanthemums and lilies fill a small plant stand, creating a colorful focal point.*

RIGHT *Decorated clay and wooden pots, and a rustic wooden basket, all help to create variety and interest in small-space gardening.*

*T*HE DAYS WHEN *container gardening meant choosing between a clay and a plastic flowerpot are gone. Even the most basic garden center now has a good range of competitively priced pots, troughs, and planters to choose from, while specialist craftspeople and importers will supply you with anything from amazingly authentic-looking fiberglass copies of antique lead troughs and terracotta urns to richly glazed Vietnamese and Provençal pots. Many of these containers are so decorative that there is a risk of overdoing the effect when using them. Generally, you should aim for a simple architectural effect rather than a glorious profusion.*

Many imported terracotta pots are inexpensive and very decorative, but not frost-proof. They can be used for summer plants, but must be brought indoors for the winter. In cold areas it is best to buy terracotta that has been fired at very high temperatures to withstand frost damage. If you use saucers under pots in summer, it is vital to remove them in late fall because even the toughest pot will crack if left standing in frozen water. Lining decorative pots with

BELOW *A rustic wooden trough makes an excellent home in spring for dwarf hebes, polyanthus, and scillas, the latter replaced in summer and fall with a seasonal display.*

slightly smaller plastic pots avoids having to discard spring flowers

that are still looking good to get the summer plants established.

Reclamation yards are excellent sources for unusual

containers, especially when you are looking for something fairly

large as a focal point. They are also good places to find plinths,

columns, and other architectural items. Look for smaller

containers in junk stores and flea markets – an old tin bath with

a hole in it is useless for its original purpose but can look great

when planted with spring bulbs, and a metal bottle-carrier will

hold pots of flowering plants just as easily as bottles.

TOP Even a growing bag assumes designer
status when its contents are color-coordinated.

ABOVE Simple terracotta pots can be painted
to add interest to any planting display, as these
little pots of marigolds demonstrate.

27

CLASSIC CONTAINERS

A lushly planted classic urn is all that is needed to give a small space both drama and elegance. Whether set against a backdrop of unadorned brick or stone, or backed by a mass of climbing plants, its outline will furnish its surroundings and draw the eye. It adds instant height and structure to a garden, and a sense of the theatrical.

SOME CONTAINERS are very much secondary to the plants that grow in them, but this should not be the case when using classic containers, such as stone urns. These are beautiful objects on their own, and can even be used unplanted as sculptures during the winter. In the spring, densely planted with tulips (*Tulipa*), an urn is a dramatic focal point while luxuriant summer plants will soften its outline but still make sure that it is the center of attention. To be best admired, the urn should be placed at eye-level on a ledge or plinth – at ground level its outline is too easily lost amid its surroundings.

The planting can take the form of eye-catching feature plants (see pages 122-3), foliage plants (see pages 124-5), or a mixture of trailing plants (see pages 126-8) that drape attractively over the rim of the container. Make sure the planting colors and textures complement the style of the pot.

When planting the urn for summer, choose a central plant that has enough drama of its own not to be overwhelmed by its container. It should grow to the same height as that of the urn and spread well over its sides, although more upright plants can be used in combination with trailing plants that provide width. It is essential to water the urns daily and to fertilize and deadhead the plants regularly – a compelling visual statement such as a classic urn will inevitably be a prominent focal point and neglect will be very noticeable.

PLANTING A GRAND URN

Grand containers deserve to be filled with equally grand plants. An exuberant Datura (syn. Brugmansia) spills out of this container and towers above all the other plants in the border. The rounded shape created by the various leaves and flowers is the perfect contrast to the urn in which they are planted. The plants used for this display are shown below.

Datura (syn. Brugmansia)   **Helichrysum**   **Salvia patens 'Cambridge'**   **Verbena**

PLANTING A SUMMER POT

This impressive container makes a very dramatic statement among the surrounding greenery. The plants used are:

Melianthus major

Helichrysum microphyllum

Pelargonium 'Voodoo'

Salvia 'Raspberry Royale'

Argyranthemum 'Flamingo'

UNUSUAL CONTAINERS

The adventurous gardener may find the choice of pots available at most garden centers rather ordinary, while the more unusual commercially available alternatives are frequently very expensive. There are, however, plenty of wonderful containers to be found in thrift shops, reclamation yards, and even in your own attic. Gardening is, after all, an expression of each individual's creativity and this does not need to be limited to your choice of plants. Quirky containers are fun, eye-catching, and original.

WHEN WE BUY new containers for the garden we expect them to be in perfect condition and to prove durable. This does not need to be the case with unusual containers, which are frequently objects that have been discarded because they no longer fulfill their original function. They may only last two or three seasons before they finally collapse, but in the meantime you will have had the pleasure of an inexpensive container and you can enjoy a more creative form of recycling than a visit to the waste-management center.

A woven basket that has lost its handle is useless for carrying things, but it is charming as a moss-lined container for alpine strawberries or pinks (*Dianthus*). An old black saucepan, rusted through at the bottom, is an appropriate container for otherwise invasive mint (*Mentha*) when placed next to the kitchen door, and a wooden wheelbarrow, discarded because its wheel wobbles and it can hardly be lifted, becomes a decorative planter.

Just because you have never seen something used as a container before does not mean it can't do the job. Provided you create some drainage holes and there is room for a sufficient depth of soil, practically anything can become a planter. However, keep in mind that unusual does not have to mean tacky – old car tires and bedpans or disused toilets work as containers but they seldom look decorative, so keep your aesthetic sensibilities about you when searching for something new.

TOP *An unusual sculpted animal head is adorned with ferns and grasses.*

LEFT *Disused cooking pots make ideal planters for small spring bulbs.*

RIGHT *A wheelbarrow makes a charming feature in a small courtyard when filled with small succulents.*

OPPOSITE PAGE *The open drawers of an eclectic mixture of discarded furniture create a novel form of tiered planting in a small backyard.*

FEATURE CONTAINERS

When strikingly planted, one grand, large-scale container can form the centerpiece of a small space and inspire the rest of the planting. It can even be the only significant planting in an area that otherwise consists of varied textures of hard landscaping, such as stone, brick, or paving that will become softened in time by moss and creeping plants. Raising the container above the level of the surrounding planting will often increase the impact.

PROBLEM CORNERS or difficult spaces can become a positive asset in the small garden when plants and containers are imaginatively combined. Allow yourself to be inspired by other people's bright ideas and keep a notebook handy to record particularly good plant combinations or inspired marriages of plants and containers. Planting schemes from famous gardens can be scaled down effectively.

Even the smallest space can take one large, dramatic plant. This generally works best when the plant has architectural or textured foliage or flowers. Hostas (*Hosta*), ferns, cordylines (*Cordyline*), and New Zealand flax (*Phormium*) all have handsome foliage; lilies (*Lilium*), Angel's trumpets (*Datura*), and peonies (*Paeonia*) have glorious flowers; and the globe artichoke (*Cynara scolymus*) has serrated silver-gray foliage and magnificent, purple thistle-like flowers.

TOP LEFT *The shimmering leaves of* Helichrysum petiolare *catch the light.*

LEFT *A bowl of succulents on top of a stone column makes a bold statement.*

ABOVE AND FACING PAGE *Large containers of architectural plants stand out dramatically from the surrounding greenery, as with the variegated-leaved hosta (above) and the fern (right).*

TROUGHS

Troughs are often the ideal planters for narrow spaces, including windowsills and balconies. An attractive view can be framed with colorful low-growing plants, while a less decorative outlook can be masked by more abundant foliage and flowers. When selecting your plants, choose some that are fragrant so their scent will waft through an open door or window.

TROUGHS COME in many forms, including wood, stone, pottery, and metal. Choose colors and textures of container that are appropriate for the setting. If your budget will not extend to expensive containers, why not consider recycling household containers instead? The most interesting gardens often feature containers that have been adapted from their original purpose. While many of these containers have previously been used as the manufacturers intended, it is also possible to buy them new and to use them in the garden from the start. Styrofoam troughs, like those used for wallpapering, are one example. They are inexpensive and available from decorating stores, easy to paint, and have the added benefit of being very lightweight, making them ideal for roof gardens and balconies where weight can be a serious consideration. Most of the manufacturers of these troughs have realized that they have an alternative use in the garden, so have marked the base of the trough to show where drainage holes should be made.

Although lacking the inherent strength of most containers, styrofoam is actually a very plant-friendly material because it absorbs and retains warmth from the sun and therefore stimulates good root growth.

PREPARING A STYROFOAM TROUGH

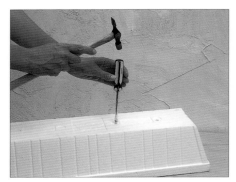

1 *Turn the trough upside down and use a hammer and screwdriver to pierce the drainage holes following the manufacturer's markings. If there are no markings, make eight holes in two parallel lines along the base.*

2 *Place the trough on a protected work surface and paint the sides and the base. Allow to dry, then paint the rim and the inside to below soil level. You can use latex paint, but red oxide paint gives a more durable finish.*

ABOVE *Filled with summer-flowering gazanias and portulacas, this styrofoam trough has been painted terracotta, successfully disguising its more humble origins. Adding a few little treasures, such as these shells, increases the decorative effect.*

RIGHT *Echeverias fill a long concrete trough, their flowers spilling over and softening its outlines. Daisylike plants (Erigeron karvinskianus) also help to create a natural look.*

SMALL CONTAINERS

While small containers can go unnoticed in a large garden, they are essential components of the small garden, terraced patio, or balcony. Here, every flowerpot and planter should be chosen to make a positive contribution to the scene, and the plants changed seasonally for a continuous display, or selected so they will look good throughout the year. For maximum impact, plant in blocks of color instead of mixed colors, and group the pots together rather than position them individually.

IN A SMALL SPACE, containers are an important part of the architecture and "furniture" of the garden. They help to create the mood – strong architectural shapes, even on a small scale, will give the space formality; rustic planters convey a more simple garden atmosphere; and brightly glazed or painted pots can transform an urban yard into a corner of the Mediterranean.

A formal space needs little more than evergreen topiary softened here or there with pots of one variety of seasonal flower in a single color. For example, a white theme might feature pansies (*Viola × wittrockiana*) in the winter, narcissi (*Narcissus*) in the spring, tobacco plants (*Nicotiana*) in the summer and cyclamen (*Cyclamen*) in the fall. The scale can be as small as needed to suit the space; it can even be small enough to display on a tabletop, with home-grown compact varieties of evergreens or herbs that have been pruned to shape and small-leaved ivies (*Hedera*) trained over frames.

The less formal space is easily given a seasonal change of color and style. Plastic flowerpots of plants can be slipped inside your containers so there is no need to dig them up before re-planting the container. Simply remove the plastic pot and tuck it out of sight so the plant can die back naturally.

RIGHT *Dramatically colored black grass (Ophiopogon 'Nigrescens') is teamed with a dark Sempervivum. Hebe and a pale pink viola provide contrast.*

RIGHT AND FAR RIGHT
*Use of alpine, miniature,
and compact varieties of
plants such as these will
ensure that the containers
are not swamped by their
contents.*

RIGHT *A bark basket, with
its evocative woodland
associations, is the perfect
complement to the lilies of
the valley (Convallaria
majalis) nestled in
a bed of moss.*

MINIATURE DISPLAYS

As children, many of us enjoyed creating miniature gardens. These were usually of a very temporary nature, made out of mosses, twigs, and little flowers, but this should not be a form of gardening that is abandoned with maturity – it is something that can still be enjoyed by using a more sophisticated construction. A carefully chosen shallow container planted with alpine and other little plants becomes a miniature landscape full of fascinating detail, which would be unnoticed if the same plants were growing at ground level.

THIS FORM of gardening is accessible to practically anyone because it only needs the tiniest of spaces – a windowsill or tabletop is sufficient. Miniature displays can be created by planting a single container with a group of plants or by planting choice specimens in individual pots and grouping them together. Either way you will have plants that you can maintain and admire up close.

When grouping plants in a single container it works best when the container used is long and shallow, so it is in scale with the plants; this will help you create a miniature landscape, rather than just a mixed planting. Before removing the plants from the pots in which they were grown, experiment with their positions within your chosen container. Once you are happy with their relationship to one another, plant them firmly in good-quality potting soil with added slow-release fertilizer. When planting a spring, fall, or winter garden, surround the plants with moss; a summer garden should have coarse sand or gravel around the plants. Both of these soil coverings are decorative and also help to retain moisture and prevent the soil from being splashed onto the leaves and flowers during watering. Individual specimen plants will also look better than ever when given this treatment.

RIGHT *A miniature terracotta trough (shown opposite with a summer display) is filled in spring with country garden favorites, such as primroses and violas.*

PLANTING A MINIATURE SUMMER DISPLAY

A small stone trough or wooden container makes the ideal miniature garden because it looks good when placed at eye-level on a tabletop or windowsill. It requires careful composition – choose plants whose foliage and flowers complement each another, like the summer-flowering plants shown below. Alternatively, a container filled with a single type of flower, such as snowdrops (Galanthus) in the early spring or houseleeks (Sempervivum) in the summer, looks very striking, or you can create a mixed planting found in the garden center, such as rare or unusual plants that would be overlooked if planted in the borders.

PLANTS FOR THE MINIATURE SUMMER DISPLAY

Dianthus 'Nyewoods Cream'   **Drosanthemum hispidum**   **Geranium cinereum**   **Sisyrinchium bellum**

HANGING CONTAINERS

Hanging containers are an invaluable asset when gardening in a small space. While other containers use the horizontal or vertical surfaces of the garden, hanging containers create another dimension by using the airspace.

You can create mixed plantings or use a single variety of flower to make a bold statement. When space is limited, hanging baskets can even be used to grow herbs and miniature vegetables, such as cherry tomatoes, lettuces, and eggplants.

HANGING BASKETS are really miniature gardens in their own right, with the great advantage that you have more control over the position, soil conditions, and plants than in most other types of gardening. They are fairly labor-intensive, because they need regular watering and fertilizing to ensure a long-lasting display of flowers and foliage, but hanging baskets will reward you with a concentration of color that can be much more elusive elsewhere in your garden.

There was a time when hanging baskets were purely for summer display; filled with colorful, tender plants, they brightened the garden for a few

Thymus **Rosmarinus** **Tropaeolum** **Ocimum basilicum**

PLANTING A HERBAL HANGING BASKET

A densely planted basket of herbs positioned close to a kitchen door (above) is both attractive and useful. Regular picking will keep the herbs growing strong and provide aromatic ingredients for your cooking. The inclusion of a plant with edible flowers, such as nasturtium (Tropaeolum), gives the basket an extra element of color. Many colors of nasturtium are now available – choose from red, orange, yellow, apricot, and peach.

PLANTING AN ALL-YEAR HANGING BASKET

We tend to think of hanging baskets as a summer feature, but when planted with evergreens and seasonal color, they can continue to look good throughout the year. A mixture of upright, decorative ferns, trailing evergreen ivy (Hedera), periwinkle (Vinca), and pansies (Viola) is the basic planting scheme for this hanging basket (below). The small-flowered blue pansies will bloom over many months, provided that they are regularly deadheaded and occasionally cut back to encourage fresh new growth. Their color will accentuate the blue periwinkle flowers.

Polypodium vulgare

Dryopteris erythrosora

Cyrtomium fortunei

Vinca minor

Viola x *wittrockiana*

months. Now, they are increasingly filled with seasonal plants for spring and fall displays and, in milder areas or sheltered corners, hanging baskets can be used to relieve the winter gloom. Garden centers stock many suitable plants throughout the year and some even sell color-themed selections which are ready for planting. This is often a good starting point for the beginner because the plants have been chosen for their suitability in hanging baskets.

It is important to have a strong, secure bracket for a hanging basket – a recently watered basket filled with plants can be very heavy and could inflict serious damage if it falls. For a colorful display, it is best to position the bracket where the basket will be in the sun for some part of the day. However, if this is not possible, there are plants that will flower happily in shade and when mixed with variegated foliage they can still provide a splash of color – use violets (*Viola*), pansies (*Viola* × *wittrockiana*), and miniature bulbs during the cooler months and busy lizzies (*Impatiens*) throughout the summer.

DOORWAYS & STEPS

If the truth is known, many of us are fair-weather

gardeners, and there are parts of the garden which we

only visit when the sun shines. However, doorways

and steps do not fall into this category – these are

used daily, so planting should be planned accordingly.

Steps make a wonderful

showcase for pots of

plants that are looking

their best, because the

flowers can be admired

from many angles, while

a doorway provides the perfect frame for climbers.

ABOVE *Fuchsia and clematis mingle together in a courtyard entrance. Many varieties of fuchsia, and some clematis, will do well even in partial shade.*

RIGHT *Areas with little planting space can still support an astonishing variety of plants, using climbers on walls and containers on every ledge and step.*

CLIMBING PLANTS, *hanging baskets, and wall pots can all be used to frame a door, and if you incorporate evergreen and hardy plants there will always be something of interest. An evergreen clematis, such as* C. cirrhosa, *will flower in midwinter as its bronze foliage twines among the bare stems of a climbing rose; a hanging basket filled with ferns will look good in the coldest weather; and a winter display of ivies* (Hedera) *and pansies* (Viola x wittrockiana) *will keep a wall pot looking colorful. Given the limitations of space, choose your climbing plants carefully – they should be reasonably compact, flower over a long period, and have a good fragrance. Plants that might go unnoticed elsewhere disclose their charms when placed on steps. Pots of snowdrops* (Galanthus) *and hellebores are a delight with their delicate flowers, which bloom in winter. In summer, aromatic herbs and scented flowers thrive on the heat radiated by sun-drenched steps, and the fragrance they release will be especially intense. Whatever the season, pots grouped around a doorway and on steps look great, but keep in mind you still need to have access to the house!*

BELOW *A small gate, overhung by climbers on a pergola, is almost obscured by a lush planting of* Crocosmia *on the steps leading up to it.*

FACING PAGE *Restrained formality has turned a small courtyard, and the steps leading down to it, into an elegant formal garden, with clipped boxwood balls, neat standards of bay and smart edgings of petunias.*

INFORMAL DOORWAYS

You need only read the phrase 'roses round the door' to conjure up a picture of an earthly paradise where all is beauty without and domestic harmony within. Although the reality may be more prosaic, it is undoubtedly true that plants growing around and over a doorway are nearly always decorative and a gentle pleasure for the occupants and their visitors.

CERTAIN PRACTICALITIES must be kept in mind when selecting plants to grow next to or around a doorway, especially when planting in a restricted space. Standard and topiary plants should be above or below face level, otherwise they are likely to inflict damage upon, or be damaged by, those who pass by. Lush growth is desirable around informal doorways but rampant plants can be more of an impediment than a pleasure and will need frequent pruning and tying. Stems of tall, flowering plants should be well-supported or they are likely to be broken as they are brushed against. If you are using canes to support plants, be sure to slip protective covers over the ends to prevent visitors damaging their eyes when they stoop to admire your handiwork.

When choosing climbers, select varieties that flower for as long as possible and plant two or three different climbing plants together to lengthen the flowering season. If possible, include an evergreen or a climber that bears berries or fruit.

Scent is an important consideration when planting around a doorway. This is a place where people tend to linger and it is made more enjoyable when surrounded by fragrant plants. Herbs have aromatic foliage that smells strongest when brushed against or crushed.

LEFT *Evergreen holly and ivy provide subtle winter color next to a painted door.*

RIGHT *Scented lilies (Lilium 'Casablanca'), on both sides of a doorway, make an attractive feature.*

ABOVE *An ornamental bracket positioned beside a doorway supports a hanging basket of cascading white and blue lobelia, Scaevola, and Convolvulus sabatius. With an occasional trim and regular fertilizing, this basket will continue to flower into the fall.*

Plant the herbs in pots and in crevices in the paving surrounding a door. Choose varieties of climber that are strongly scented, and be sure to include plants that release their fragrance in the evening, such as lilies (*Lilium*) and night-scented stocks (*Matthiola*). Large-flowered tall plants, such as lilies, need staking (below).

When deciding on a color scheme, the effect will be more coherent if you limit the palette. A single-color theme will lend elegance to a doorway, no matter how informal it may be. If the door is painted, choose flowering plants and foliage to complement or contrast with the paint color, because the door is central to the design and should not be disregarded. Unpainted or weathered wooden doors generally have a softer appearance and look good surrounded with muted colors, such as soft blues, pinks, and purples.

While the formal doorway generally relies on symmetrical and disciplined planting, this is not the case with the informal doorway – here, lack of symmetry can contribute to the charm and planting can be on many levels above, around, and on both sides of the door. Use climbers over and around the doorway, with hanging baskets and wall-mounted pots for high-level displays. When using hanging baskets in this situation, it is generally advisable to hang them to one side of the door rather than directly above the entrance – because they need frequent watering, this can result in unwelcome drips on those who pass underneath. Plant abundantly on either side of the door using pots and planters of various sizes filled with a combination of tall and trailing plants.

STAKING LILIES

1 *Place some drainage material in the base of the pot and half-fill it with potting soil.*

2 *Add a layer of sand to ensure free drainage, and position the bulbs evenly.*

3 *Cover with more potting soil. Push the stakes firmly into the soil at regular intervals.*

4 *As the plants grow, tie the foliage loosely to the stakes with soft string.*

ABOVE *Continuing the white theme used above, large pots on each side of the doorway are planted with sweetly scented tobacco plants (Nicotiana) against a backdrop of mopheaded hydrangeas.*

FORMAL DOORWAYS

The most effective planting is planned to complement the style of its architectural setting, and there are many doorways where formal containers filled with evergreen shrubs are more appropriate to the house and more to the taste of the occupants than flower-filled pots, which are labor-intensive and relatively short-lived.

WHILE SYMMETRY can be difficult to achieve in less formal settings, it is an easy way to add drama and style to formal entrances. Pots of topiary are a popular choice, and although they can be an expensive initial investment, they are very undemanding and look good throughout the year. Several alternatives to topiary are equally suitable for formal situations. Matched pairs of plants placed on both sides of a doorway can make a striking impression – for example, white mopheaded hydrangeas (*Hydrangea*), small mock topiary pots of

pansies (above) or grape hyacinths (*Muscari*), or more architectural foliage plants, such as cordylines (*Cordyline*) and standard bays (*Laurus nobilis*).

In general, when choosing plants for formal doorways, you cannot buy small plants and wait for them to grow. Instead, be guided by the size of the containers when you choose your plants – ball topiary and shrubs should be as tall and as wide as the container; pyramids should be one-and-a-half times the height of the container; and the stem and head of a standard should be at least double the height of the container. If

mature topiary is beyond your budget, but you want to achieve a similar effect, you can use wire topiary frames or planters topped with obelisks and train evergreen climbers over the frame – the frames and obelisks have a decorative architectural quality that will contribute to the formality of the doorway while the plants grow.

FACING PAGE *Grouping foliage plants makes a bold statement. Use contrasts of form and texture, as here. Boxwood (Buxus sempervirens), clipped into a ball, creates a foil for large fern and hosta leaves.*

TRAINING SHRUBS

Boxwood (*Buxus sempervirens*) is the ideal shrub for the beginner to use for topiary. It is very easy to grow, and once established puts on a lot of dense growth each season, which can be clipped into simple balls or pyramids. Initial success will inspire you to try more adventurous shapes.

ABOVE AND RIGHT *Regular clipping of new growth during the growing season is the best way to ensure a well-shaped shrub. Irregular pruning can eventually result in straggly growth, which spoils the dense outline of the topiary.*

ABOVE *Clip pairs of boxwood shrubs into symmetrical shapes and place on both sides of a door for a simple, elegant effect.*

HOT-COLORED BASKETS

Vibrantly colored flowers seem to absorb and radiate the heat of the summer garden, and even on a dull day their intense hues will make an impact. These are cheerful, extrovert flowers, and used in a hanging basket they will dominate a small space like an aerial exclamation mark and set the mood for the rest of the garden. Busy lizzies (right), petunias, nasturtiums, and trailing geraniums are all good candidates for such a display.

Hot-colored flowers are generally sun-loving and you will have no difficulty finding suitable plants for a sunny position. Ivy-leafed geraniums are available in brilliant cerise, magenta, and dark crimson, as well as more subtle shades, and they look wonderful with petunias and verbenas in bright colors. The smaller-flowered tumbling petunias are particularly good in hanging baskets and so prolific at flowering that they can be used on their own. For real drama you can mix what are conventionally thought of as clashing colors – putting scarlet, purple, orange, and cerise together may seem risky, but in reality it looks fantastic, provided that the rest of your garden can match such a positive statement. These strong colors work particularly well with an architectural setting as a backdrop.

For a shady garden, the pansy (*Viola × wittrockiana*) and busy lizzie (*Impatiens*) are perfect for hanging. Both prefer shade and a hanging basket of either flower will establish quickly and add color in an area that usually relies on foliage plants and pale-hued flowers.

ABOVE AND RIGHT *Vibrant colors are the hallmark of busy lizzies (Impatiens), which make superb plants for hanging baskets, thriving in either partial shade or sun.*

PLANTING A HANGING BASKET

1 *Line the basket with moss, partially fill with potting soil, add some water-retaining crystals, and start to plant.*

Hanging baskets come in various sizes, but they will all be much larger when fully planted, so keep this in mind when purchasing an appropriately sized container. You can buy preformed liners or you can line the basket with moss. Of the two, moss is the better option because it provides good insulation from drying winds and retains moisture well. It also looks more natural and it is easy to push the plants through the sides of the basket to make a more rounded outline when planted.

If you include a small amount of water-retaining crystals in the soil mix for the basket, you can reduce the amount of watering needed. Remember when planting the basket that the plants will spread considerably when fully grown; nevertheless, err on the generous side – nothing looks worse than a sparse hanging basket. It will take a month or so for the hanging basket to look its best. The one above was photographed two weeks after planting; the blue and silver hanging basket on page 53 was photographed three weeks after. Not all plants will fill out as quickly as others. See pages 126-129 for suitable plants.

2 *Continue to add the plants, making sure that some are pushed through the sides of the basket, and fill with soil.*

3 *Neaten the planting, trimming off any straggling shoots with a pair of sharp scissors, to create a balanced shape.*

PLANTS FOR THE YELLOW AND RED DISPLAY
Shades of yellow and red, backed by green foliage, create a hot-colored display using the plants shown below.

FROM LEFT TO RIGHT *Sedum sieboldii, Coreopsis grandiflora, Begonia, yellow summer pansies (Viola sp.), red summer pansies (Viola sp.), Solenostemon scutellarioides, Hedera helix, and dwarf chrysanthemum.*

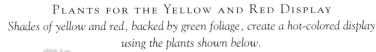

THEMED BASKETS

Hanging baskets are among the most colorful displays for the garden, as well as the most space-saving, because they can be hung from any sturdy overhead structure. Although hanging baskets can look marvelous when they are a kaleidoscope of color, a more sophisticated look is achieved when the baskets are color-themed.

YOU CAN create color contrasts or harmonies with any planting scheme, according to the situation you envisage for the baskets. They look impressive displayed as a pair on both sides of a doorway, but asymmetric displays also work well in limited spaces. Where there is more than one hanging basket in an area, it is usually best to plant each one with the same selection of plants or they may look muddled. Alternatively, each basket can be planted with a single color to create blocks of color – this is very effective against a background of dark foliage.

Choosing colors that go well together from a range of plants with more or less the same flowering season can prove tricky, particularly when the habit of the plant is critical, too. For hanging baskets, the ideal plants have a lax habit, fairly rapid growth, and a long flowering season. It is now possible to buy color-themed collections of hanging basket plants from the garden center or nursery, and although they are not always the most exciting selection of plants, they are a good starting point and can easily be enlivened with a few imaginative flourishes of your own.

PLANTS FOR THE PINK AND MAUVE DISPLAY
The plants below, a mixture of annuals and perennials, have been used to create the display shown above.
FROM LEFT TO RIGHT *Lavender stoechas 'Papillon;' Hedera; Helichrysum petiolare 'Aurea;' Dianthus; Pelargonium; New Guinea Impatiens; Fuchsia; and Viola × wittrockiana.*

PLANTS FOR THE BLUE AND SILVER DISPLAY

Again, a mixture of annuals and perennials (below) in complementary colors has been used to create the display above, with blue pansies predominating. FROM LEFT TO RIGHT *Salvia officinalis; Hedera; Viola × wittrockiana; Salvia farinacea; Senecio maritima; Viola × wittrockiana; Helichrysum microphyllum.*

FOLIAGE STEPS

Steps are a great asset in the small garden. They mark a change of levels, which always makes a space more interesting, and they provide a tiered display area that shows off plants to great advantage. Using foliage plants on steps can be as simple as allowing ivy (Hedera) to cascade down from surrounding walls, or they can be the setting for splendid architectural plants or topiary and become a focal point of the garden.

WITH FOLIAGE planting it is easy to keep steps looking interesting all year round, whatever your chosen style of gardening. Informal steps are often made from a mixture of materials – bricks, stone, tiles, slates, and even wood – and there are usually crevices into which you can tuck creeping plants such as sedum, sempervivum, *Arisarum,* and saxifrage that will spread and soften the whole

ABOVE *Small grasses or grass-like plants make a neat edging to steps.*

area. This is particularly useful where space is very limited and there isn't enough room to place pots on the steps.

In formal settings the choice of containers is critical. A miscellaneous collection of pots of varying materials is not appropriate because they will look too casual for the effect you are trying to create. Simple terracotta pots lined up on either side of the steps will be far more effective than a hodgepodge of pots and planters.

When it comes to formal planting, topiary, standards, architectural, and compact evergreen shrubs all look good, but you don't have to restrict yourself to the usual boxwood (*Buxus sempervirens*), bay (*Laurus nobilis*), and ivy (*Hedera*) – many other more unusual varieties of plants are worth considering. The star jasmine (*Trachelospermum diffusum*) is a handsome, evergreen climbing plant with glossy, green leaves that become tinged with red in winter, and it has the added bonus of small, sweetly scented white flowers in the summer. Trained onto a frame, it is a good addition to sunny steps, as are herbs, such as rosemary (*Rosmarinus*), cotton lavender (*Santolina*), and wormwood (*Artemisia*).

For shadier positions, take inspiration from Japanese gardens. Glazed pots of compact bamboos, azaleas, ferns, and rhododendrons, grouped with moss and smooth river stones covering the soil around the plants, will convey a suitably lush, green atmosphere.

In exposed positions, low-growing plants are often more appropriate. Stone bowls or troughs of sempervivums or sedums have an interesting textural quality and will tolerate a wide range of weather conditions.

If you enjoy scent, remember that there are some scented plants which also have handsome foliage. Neatly clipped artemisia (see page 56) looks good in terracotta pots and is highly aromatic. Equally aromatic is the slow-growing Christmas boxwood (*Sarcococca*), which looks attractive planted in groups.

ABOVE *Wide steps leading to a veranda create an opportunity for a tiered display of handsome foliage plants, including boxwood topiary (a spiral is shown on the facing page, above) and a tender lemon tree (Citrus sp.).*

LEFT *Narrow steps can be flanked with containers of handsome foliage plants, such as agaves or yuccas.*

SCENTED STEPS

The fragrance released by plants when you brush against them is highly evocative; it can conjure up memories of childhood, recollections of other gardens, and reminders of hot summer vacations. Our sense of smell connects directly to our emotions, which is why we react with feeling to smells that are pleasant and unpleasant. Scented plants growing beside steps create a fragrant corridor that will envelop all those who pass.

WITHIN THE CONFINES of a small garden, patio, or balcony, fragrant plants can work their magic to maximum effect, filling the air with a scent that may be lost in a larger area. By concentrating aromatic planting on steps, beside paths, and around doorways, you will be able to enjoy the scent whenever you venture outdoors.

Provided the steps are wide enough, the most effective way to use scented plants is in containers. As with other areas in the small garden, using pots and planters allows you to move the plants around so that the star performers are in the foreground while those that are past their best can be relegated to the back.

Although one generally associates scented plants with summer, there are plants with fragrant flowers or foliage that can be appreciated throughout the year. Many herbs, such as lavender (*Lavandula*), *Santolina*, thyme (*Thymus*), and rosemary (*Rosmarinus*), retain all or at least some of their aromatic foliage during the winter when they can be placed beside fragrant flowering shrubs, such as witch hazel (*Hamamelis*), *Viburnum*, and Christmas boxwood (*Sarcococca*). These shrubs can be grown in containers and kept compact by regular pruning. From early spring on, line the steps with pots of scented bulbs and fragrant wallflowers (*Cheiranthus*) and include a pot of the delicious daphne. As spring advances into early summer, the choice of aromatic plants becomes even wider as the sharp, clean scents of spring give way to the heady fragrances of summer, and the temptation to linger on the steps becomes irresistible.

LEFT *Repeat planting on steps creates greater impact than when the planting is mixed.*

TOP *A formal pot of aromatic artemisia.*

ABOVE *Scented spring-flowering bulbs provide a tiered display on a flight of steps.*

FACING PAGE *Plants that grow in more tropical regions will flourish on sunny steps.*

WALLS

Not every garden has a wall that makes a handsome architectural feature, but many have some form of enclosing structure which can be used to support plants. Brick or stone walls also offer the opportunity to use the tops for plant displays, with the added benefit that they deter intruders. Vertical planting

increases the available space immeasurably, so use it to greatest advantage, either as a support for climbers, or by putting up trellis or shelves to display repeating groups of small plants.

ABOVE A ledge provides the opportunity for container-grown plants. Here, terracotta pots filled with herbs are displayed against a backdrop of climbing foliage.

RIGHT Colorful containers of clipped boxwood and Muscari armeniacum are lined up in impressive formation along the tops of sturdy brick walls.

OST GARDENERS aspire to a walled garden, but even if that is a dream that few of us will realize, we all have gardens with at least one wall, even if it is only the external wall of our house. Any wall is an asset in a garden. In a small alleyway or on a balcony, walls are the largest planting area available, whether covered with climbers, tiered plants, wall pots, or hanging baskets. On a small terraced patio or in a courtyard, using the walls as a vertical garden frees up precious ground space for a table and chairs or a feature such as a fountain, pond, or statue.

A brick or stone wall is a wonderful background for climbing, tumbling, or trailing plants, but not all walls are made of such attractive materials – some may be in poor condition and need disguising to look their best. Faced with this type of problem, a good solution is to paint the wall in a dark color and then cover the surface with trellis. The wall will fade unobtrusively into the background and the trellis will provide a secure structure

BELOW *Wall pots, attached to trellis, can make a colorful display that changes with the seasons. Here,* Primula obconica *and ferns create a splash of color.*

FACING PAGE *(Top) A mask wall mount, capped with bright busy lizzies, creates a focal point on a brick wall. (Below) In a shady spot beneath an old stone wall, clothed with climbing clematis and honeysuckle, a little display of corydalis, poppies, and ferns among old terracotta pots catches the eye.*

for attaching your plants. If you place containers on a high wall,

make sure they will not blow down and cause damage. To

increase the height of a wall or fence, consider attaching trellis to

the top. Painted a sympathetic blue or green, trellis looks good on

its own, but will also provide the perfect support for any twining

climber, such as honeysuckle or clematis.

AURICULA THEATER

Even in the smallest garden it is possible for plants to flower unseen. Tucked under the foliage of larger plants or overwhelmed by a vigorous neighbor, their beauty can be overlooked when they flower close to the ground. Placing decorative plants at eye-level by displaying them on shelves or other wall-mounted features, such as an old garden sieve, makes it possible to appreciate them fully when they are at their most beautiful.

AURICULA (*Primula auricula*) theaters first became popular in eighteenth-century England. Immigrant Flemish weavers would hold 'Primrose Feasts' where they would display their prize plants on black-painted shelves which would emphasize the dramatic markings of the auriculas. Fashionable society soon took up the hobby, and enthusiasts built elaborate theaters draped with black velvet with reflecting mirrors and lamplight which they filled with prize auriculas to impress their guests and cause envy among their neighbors. Although much of this was pure conceit, there was a certain practicality because many of the dramatically marked varieties of auricula need to be fully sheltered from wind and rain to keep their flowers in good condition.

Nowadays few gardeners have the space or time to devote an area of the garden to a single variety of plant that flowers for just one month in the late spring, but a small area of wall space that can be used to display plants when they are in their prime is feasible even in the smallest of gardens. The 'theater' can be as simple as a timber shelf mounted on brackets, but if you prefer something more decorative you could make or buy a pretty, unpainted pine shelf unit and paint it with black wood

preservative before mounting it on the wall. Old terracotta pots used as sleeves for plastic pots will add an appropriate finishing touch.

Whatever form your 'theater' takes, you will be able to use it throughout the year to display your small treasures. From the beginning of the year when there will be snowdrops (*Galanthus*), celandines (*Chelidonium*), and crocus (*Crocus*), through the abundance of spring and summer to the rich colors of fall cyclamen (*Cyclamen*) and heathers (*Erica, Calluna* and *Daboecia*), there will be an ever-changing tableau to admire and enjoy.

DIVIDING AURICULA PLANTS

To ensure a continuing display of healthy auricula plants it is advisable to split the plants after flowering. The young plants will quickly establish themselves and be ready to flower the following year.

1 *Gently remove the auricula plant from its pot, shake away some of the soil, and carefully separate the plantlets from one another by teasing the roots apart.*

2 *Plant the young plantlets in individual pots filled with a mixture of two parts compost to one part coarse grit. Water well and stand in a cool position for the summer.*

An old shelf unit is painted black and given a new lease of life as an auricula theater. Top row: 'Marie Creuse' and 'Walton'; second row: 'Sirius' and 'Old Mustard'; third row: 'Marie Creuse' and 'Sandwood Bay'.

ABOVE *Auricula plants are very tough and do not need a great deal of attention. Originally alpine plants, they still retain their inherent vigor. Breeders have created many varieties, including this pretty blue 'Walton'.*

ABOVE *'Sirius' is a variety of auricula particularly recommended to the beginner. It is very easy to grow and its stunning buff and plum flowers are produced in great abundance.*

REPEATING WALL POTS

One of the advantages of a small garden is that the boundaries of a patio

are often walls or fences which can be used for additional planting. Just as a

room benefits from decoration on the walls as well as the furniture on the floor,

so a patio becomes much more interesting if the pots are not only sited at ground

level but also up, and on top of, walls and fences. This creates a complete

surrounding of color and texture.

ALTHOUGH WALLS ARE ideal supports for climbing plants, they can create the perfect planting opportunity for equally striking displays of perennials and annuals. You will enhance the impact of such a display if you orchestrate a series of containers, either along the top of a wall or in pots attached to a trellis, with similar plantings, like the repeating pots of lavender on the wall top, below, or the little terracotta pots of pansies and violas beneath them. Trailing plants, such as decorative small-leaved ivies, can be used both to soften the outline of the pots and to clamber up the wall or trellis unaided. Make sure the wall or fence is in good condition, and paint any wood with preservative at regular intervals.

Trellis makes an ideal frame for climbing plants in troughs at ground level and also provides fixing points for wall pots to create a lush effect while the climbing plants are still establishing themselves. Wall-top troughs and pots may need to be secured in place with brackets (see Garden Jobs, page 116-7) to make sure they don't become dislodged.

LEFT *Alternating troughs of lavender (Lavandula) and pots of variegated ivy (Hedera) soften this wall top and also act as a deterrent to intruders.*

RIGHT *This trellis-covered wall is softened by evergreen climbing plants and ivy (Hedera) which look good throughout the year. They are further enhanced by seasonal splashes of color in the other wall pots, which are planted with petunias in shades of blue and purple.*

TERRACOTTA WALL POTS

Unless you own a mature garden you will probably have an area of bare wall or fence that can be greatly improved by the addition of terracotta wall pots. Even when empty these have a decorative quality, and with seasonal plantings they can be used to enliven an otherwise dull area with color and lush foliage. You can also choose evergreen plants for a display that looks good in every season, perhaps adding a splash of color with a flowering plant such as a pansy or viola.

I T IS ESSENTIAL to fix terracotta wall pots securely to the wall or fence because they are weighty objects. Don't be tempted to hang a pot on a convenient nail – with the addition of compost and plants, and the increased weight from watering, you will almost certainly go out one morning to find your pot reduced to a heap of shards, scattered compost, and broken plants.

When planting the pot, be sure to use a compost that is specially formulated for containers, preferably with an added moisture-retaining gel – terracotta pots dry out far quicker than plastic because the water is absorbed by the clay and evaporates from its surface.

To look their best, these pots need careful planting and regular attention. Choose plants that do well in containers and bear in mind that if the wall pot is in a sunny position it will get very hot at times in the summer when the heat radiates off the surface behind it as well as shines directly on the pot. Therefore there is no point in choosing a plant that wilts in direct sunlight and likes a moist root run. If you are uncertain about which plants to select, ask the garden center for advice or look for inspiration in other people's gardens. Your choice of colors should also take into account the color of the wall or fence. For instance, salmon pink petunias (*Petunia*) look good against gray stone but horrible against red brick, and variegated foliage is more noticeable than ordinary green foliage when set against a dark background.

LEFT *A pleasingly weathered wall pot is planted with an unusual pink and blue display of spring flowers. Deep pink arabis, burgundy pansies (see detail top), and violet violas are complemented by the blue grape hyacinths growing beneath the pot and the stencilled flowers on the nesting box.*

PLANTING A SUMMER WALL POT

The same pot pictured in the spring display (facing page) has been used for the far more exuberant summer planting shown here. While the shape and general appearance of the pot is a feature in the spring, it is soon hidden by plenty of luxuriant growth in the summer. To keep a pot like this looking good, it is essential to feed, water, and dead-head the plants regularly. When planning your planting, do remember to take into account the color of the backdrop – what looks great against a red brick wall can look washed out and uninspiring when placed against a pale background. If you are unsure of what to choose, strong, hot colors will have an impact in most positions.

1 *Place drainage material in the bottom of the pot and half-fill with compost. Position the* Felicia *in the center with a verbena on either side.*

2 *Plant the two helichrysum in front of the verbenas on either side of the pot and fill the central gap with the convolvulus. Add more compost.*

PLANTS FOR THE SUMMER WALL POT

Helichrysum petiolare 'Aurea'

Verbena 'Loveliness'

Felicia amelloides

Convolvulus sabatius

FLOWERY WALLS

A wall of colorful cascading flowers is a breathtaking sight and will make a real impact on a patio or balcony, or in a small garden. To look good for as long as possible walls will need a careful choice of plants and more attention than other areas of the garden, but your efforts will be amply rewarded. Making greatest use of all the available space is the chief aim of any small-space gardener. Walls are no exception, and can be imaginatively utilized to create additional impact in the garden.

WHEN SELECTING plants for your flowery walls, look for varieties that bloom for as long as possible. However ravishing a rose may look, its value in the small garden is greatly diminished if it grows rampantly and only flowers for a month: look for roses described as 'repeat flowering' and 'compact' for a manageable, long-lasting display. When planting into the soil rather than containers, extend the flowering season by mixing climbers to flower from early spring through to fall. The twiggy stems of early-flowering *Chaenomeles japonica* will support clematis scrambling through it to flower in the spring and summer. The passion flower (*Passiflora caerulea*) is fast-growing but worth considering for its lovely flowers, and it can be kept in check by cutting it hard back in the spring. Annual climbers such as the sweet pea (*Lathyrus odoratus*), morning glory (*Ipomoea*), and black-eyed susan (*Thunbergia alata*) will provide additional color through the summer.

In Spain, courtyard walls are covered from ground level to eaves with brackets holding pots of pelargoniums. This sort of repeat planting is very eye-catching and the pelargoniums thrive in the hot, dry conditions. Shelves can be used as an alternative to brackets, either wall-mounted or placed on the ground. Look for other plants that also do well in hot, dry conditions, such as begonias and nasturtiums (*Tropaeolum*), but bear in mind that these plants will still need regular feeding, watering and deadheading in order to look their best.

TOP *Climbing plants like clematis (Clematis 'Victoria', top left) and Plumbago auriculata (top right) provide a splash of color.*

LEFT *Vigorous climbing roses will swiftly cover a wall, filling the air with scent.*

RIGHT *Old-fashioned pelargoniums cover a wall in a traditional display.*

TOPIARY POTS

Topiary provides the perfect solution for the stylish low-maintenance garden. It also gives the garden structure even when other plants have died down. Slow-growing evergreen plants, such as boxwood (Buxus) and bay (Laurus nobilis), are clipped into architectural shapes and planted in terracotta pots to furnish the garden with subtle but impressive style. Faster-growing climbers, such as ivy (Hedera) and clematis, can also be trained into topiary shapes over frames and will provide a similar effect in a small space for a fraction of the cost, although they will demand slightly more attention.

THE COMBINATION of weathered terracotta and clipped foliage is especially pleasing, and when used in a small garden they can help to create a sense of perspective and space which fussier planting would clutter. You can use terracotta and topiary to play with scale and create the illusion that your garden is a fragment of a much larger garden just out of view. Many of the great classical gardens of Europe consist almost entirely of topiary, which creates a sense of green architecture more than gardening, and the principles used in these gardens are just as applicable to a small space.

Caring for a topiary garden is very simple. Regular watering and an occasional feed with a slow-release fertilizer such as bone-meal is all that is necessary, apart from pruning to maintain the shape of the plant. If you choose slow-growing plants, such as boxwood, the task of pruning will not be too arduous. This means you will feel more enthusiastic about doing the job. When pruning boxwood, save some of the longer stems and, after removing the leaves from the lower half of each stem, push them into a pot of sand. Leave in a cool place to root and you will soon be growing your own topiary.

ABOVE *In an interesting reversal of the usual form, a terracotta ball rises above a base of ivy. The background of foliage throws the shape of the terracotta ball into sharp relief.*

RIGHT *Perfect symmetry isn't necessary for an eye-catching topiary display. Here, a square pot breaks the pattern as does the conical boxwood plant which contrasts pleasingly with the other ball shapes.*

QUICK TOPIARY

Not everyone can afford to buy mature topiary, and the process of growing and training your own boxwood or bay from a small plant can take several years. If this does not appeal, you may find the ideal solution is to use quick-growing evergreen climbers, such as ivy, which can be trained over wire frames. These frames are now available at most garden centers. Ivy is undoubtedly the easiest plant to train, and the small-leafed varieties are the most suitable for this purpose.

LEFT *A conical wire frame supports a combination of ivy and clematis. The plants look decorative even though they have barely filled out the wire frame.*

RIGHT *Ivy has been trained over a ball-shaped wire frame to create some quick topiary. The ivy can be easily clipped into shape whenever it becomes too unruly.*

MAKING AN IVY BALL

Plant the ivy in a pot which is the correct size for the frame you wish to use, separate the stems of the plant and wind them around the wires to cover as much of the frame as possible.

1 *Every couple of weeks, wind the new growth around the wires until the entire frame is well covered.*

2 *At this stage all you will need to do is to clip off any new growth, and feed and water the plant regularly to keep it in good health.*

CORNERS

In large gardens, corners are often neglected or used as dumping ground for broken pots and other garden equipment. In the small garden, where space is at a premium, a more imaginative and attractive solution is needed, and it soon becomes apparent that, far from being a problem, a corner is a positive asset. Tender plants thrive in the protection offered by a

sheltered corner; it can provide an interesting setting for an architectural plant like cordyline and it is the perfect backdrop for a plinth or a garden statue.

ABOVE *A standard tree of variegated holly* (Ilex aquifolium) *brings color and light to a shady corner of the garden.*

RIGHT *A little pond in a corner of the garden allows you to grow a range of damp- and water-loving plants (see page 135).*

BELOW *Majestic Fritillaria imperialis provides a welcome splash of color in an otherwise dark corner.*

BOTTOM *An antique cloche, surrounded by low-growing perennials, makes a winter feature in a small corner.*

FILLING THE CORNERS of a small garden with plants can achieve a lushness and depth that might not otherwise be possible in such a small space. A corner is the ideal position for a large shrub or small tree. Choose a variety of tree that does not grow too large and preferably has a light leaf covering to avoid creating too much shade. An ornamental Malus or the winter-flowering cherry (Prunus subhirtella 'Autumnalis') are good choices because they are decorative and regular pruning will help keep them compact. You can underplant them with bulbs or cover the area with a pattern of stones radiating out from the stem, starting 8in (20cm) away from the base, and place pots of shade-loving plants on the stones. Hydrangeas, rhododendrons, camellias, periwinkles (Vinca), hellebores, and ferns are plants that enjoy these conditions.

A paved corner that relies entirely on container plants does not need to be a problem. By filling the corner with a deep, square container you can create a raised bed, which, when filled with good-quality soil, can be used to grow climbers to train up the walls as well as trailing plants to tumble over the sides. For a

more flexible display, group pots of various sizes together in the

corner or attach a series of graduated shelves diagonally across

the corner to create a showcase for smaller plants. A corner is

also ideal for an arbor of trellis with a corner seat beneath it —

train scented climbers over the arbor and cluster pots of aromatic

herbs and lilies on both sides to create an idyllic retreat.

ABOVE *A summer display of begonias, helichrysum, and geraniums in a symmetrically composed planting, flanked by twin standards, turns a corner into a feature.*

FOLIAGE DISPLAYS

Often neglected, foliage plays a far more important role in gardens than most of us recognize. Although it is used as a foil for more immediately attractive flowering displays, it is well worthwhile considering foliage in its own right for small gardens in particular, and especially in shady ones where it can thrive. There are many varieties, textures, and colors to choose from, and many foliage plants can be clipped into decorative topiary. Others form natural architectural shapes.

SMALL POTS of topiary – created from slow-growing evergreens such as boxwood (*Buxus sempervirens*), bay (*Laurus nobilis*), and privet (*Ligustrum*) – and false topiary, created from quick-growing evergreen climbers like ivy (*Hedera*), will fit well into a shady corner, taking up extremely little space in the garden, while providing an interesting accent to the design. Apart from fairly minimal feeding and watering (both ivy and boxwood cope well with drought), they will simply need clipping every now and then.

By combining topiary with architectural plants such as New Zealand flax (*Phormium*), fatsia (*Fatsia*), and spurge (*Euphorbia*), the foliage display can achieve an interesting mix of shape, color, and texture which will look good throughout the year – ideal for the lazy or absent gardener.

ABOVE *This table-top display demonstrates the variety of colors within the green palette. Silver, gold, and green mind-your-own-business* (Soleirolia soleirolii) *and a resting* Calamintha *provide a colorful display against a backdrop of ivy* (Hedera).

RIGHT *This shady corner is full of interesting architectural shapes, thanks to the pots of topiary ivy set against the spiky-leaved cabbage palm* (Cordyline) *and trelliswork supporting a Virginia creeper* (Parthenocissus quinquefolia).

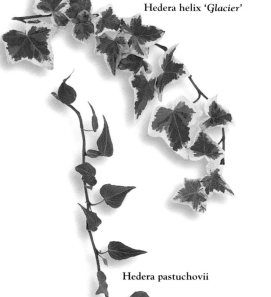

Hedera helix 'Glacier'

Hedera pastuchovii

PLANTING A FOLIAGE POT

1 *Place a few stones or broken shards of pot in the base of a suitable-sized container, and then part-fill with compost so that the soil level of the plant will be just below the top of the pot when it is filled with compost.*

2 *Place each of the plants in the pot, and then fill with potting compost, pressing it down well around the root balls of the plants. Water well to ensure that the roots are surrounded by soil.*

POTTED HERB GARDEN

When space is limited it is essential that the plants you choose are all-round performers, and this is certainly true of herbs. They are easy to grow in pots, gloriously aromatic, and impart wonderful flavors to food. Many are evergreen and respond well to pruning into topiary shapes. They are ideal plants for small spaces.

WHETHER YOUR small space is a sun-drenched courtyard, a shady balcony, or something in between, there are herbs to suit all these positions. Although most herbs will tolerate most conditions, the narrow-leaved Mediterranean herbs such as rosemary (*Rosmarinus*), thyme (*Thymus*), and sage (*Salvia*) will do best if they can enjoy the sun for part of the day, while the broad-leaved herbs from cooler climates such as mint (*Mentha*), lemon balm (*Melissa officinalis*), and sorrel (*Rumex acetosa*) prefer a more shady position. Most herbs are perennials but there are some exceptions that are worth including. Basil (*Ocimum basilicum*), the king of herbs, is a tender annual that needs lots of sheltered sunshine and moist, free-draining soil. Chervil (*Anthriscus cerefolium*) is a hardy annual with delicate, aniseed-flavored foliage that likes to grow in the shade of other herbs. Parsley (*Petroselinum crispum*) is a biennial that will grow in most places; it will last from one spring to the next but will then go to seed and have to be replaced.

TOP *A little standard rosemary* (Rosmarinus officinalis) *bush makes an ideal feature.*

ABOVE *Bay* (Laurus nobilis) *can also be trained successfully into a standard.*

FACING PAGE *Grouping herbs of varying heights together throws the different textures of the leaves into contrast.*

Mediterranean herbs like to grow in free-draining soil and will do best when transplanted into loam-based compost with added grit. Herbs are grown commercially in peat-based compost so when transplanting them it is essential to soak the compost well and gently loosen the root ball to help the roots make their way into the loam. These herbs are very tolerant of all but the most extreme cold, but they do hate to have waterlogged roots during the winter so be sure to remove any plant saucers before the cold weather arrives.

All herbs benefit from a layer of mulch on top of the compost. This helps to retain moisture during the summer, protects from extremes of cold in the winter, and prevents the soil splashing on to the leaves in wet weather.

Some of the shrubby herbs, such as rosemary, myrtle, and bay, are ideal for training into standards. Pinch out sideshoots as the plant grows, to leave a clear stem. When the required height is reached, pinch out the growing point; the lateral shoots will grow, creating a mop-headed plant.

SINGLE PLANTS IN A CORNER

Where space is very limited, or time in short supply, a single plant can be all that is needed to create an interesting focal point in a low-maintenance garden. By changing the plant or slightly re-arranging the surroundings you can ensure that the corner retains a freshness that continues to draw the attention. No matter what the scale of the corner in your garden you can furnish it in this way with eye-catching plants of an appropriate size.

FOR ANYONE with a busy life or someone who likes a nice garden but doesn't want to devote much time to pottering among the plants, a low-maintenance garden is ideal. However, although this type of garden is undemanding, it can become a bit boring. Evergreens make an excellent background but there are times when more is needed, however rampantly they climb walls and tumble over terraces. A mixture of hard surfaces also creates more interest, with stones and gravel combining well with brickwork and stone, but even when all these elements are attractively combined it can all look somewhat two-dimensional unless there is some interest in the foreground.

Planting three or four pleasing old terracotta pots with perennial plants that will look their best at different times of year will allow you to change the look of a corner in a simple but effective way. When the plants are not in use as a focal point they can be grouped with other plants in the garden until they are ready for their moment of glory. For maximum variety choose plants that are very different in shape and color. Hostas are wonderfully architectural with their ribbed leaves and many leaf colors, and those with variegated leaves are particularly good at bringing light to a dark corner. A plant with red or purple foliage is also a good choice as it contrasts nicely with the evergreens, and at least one plant that flowers profusely should be part of your selection. As a finishing touch, add a layer of mulch or gravel to the top of each pot.

ABOVE *The same corner with blue phlox (top); hosta (center) and purple sage (above).*

RIGHT *Purple-leaved oxalis (right) and begonias and pansies (far right).*

OPPOSITE *Blue-leaved* Hosta sieboldiana *'Elegans' makes a handsome feature plant.*

80

WINDOWS

Even the smallest apartment has a windowsill that can provide a place to grow a few plants. You can change the display each season to make the most of whatever is available: spring bulbs, tender annuals in summer, or evergreen foliage plants in winter. Scent plays a part, too, particularly in summer when an

open window gives you the chance to enjoy sweet-smelling pinks, tobacco plants, or night-scented stocks. You can coordinate colors in displays, and you can paint containers to enhance both the interior or exterior of your house or apartment.

ABOVE *A summer window, surrounded by wisteria, boasts a complementary display of petunias, geraniums, and helichrysum.*

RIGHT *An eye-catching winter windowbox with a colorful display of cyclamens and ornamental cabbages.*

WHETHER YOUR HOME *is a country farmhouse, a formal town house, or a city apartment, decorating your windowsills with plants can enhance your home and give pleasure to all who pass by. Ideally, the containers you use and your choice of plants should be sympathetic to the architecture of your home. A country windowsill needs just a few terracotta pots filled with old-fashioned plants, such as scented geraniums (*Pelargonium*), pinks (*Dianthus*), and auriculas (*Primula*), while you can emphasize the formality of a town house by placing matching windowboxes on each windowsill and filling them with a mixture of topiary and trailing plants with added seasonal flowering plants in a single color for a touch of brightness. In an urban apartment your windowsills may be the only garden you have, and how you choose to decorate the windowsills can be a reflection of your attitude to urban life – fashionable grasses in glazed Japanese pots for a style fiend; favorite flowers taken from friends' gardens for the reluctant urban resident; or exotic herbs and miniature vegetables for the foodie. All these and more can be grown successfully on your windowsills.*

ABOVE *By midsummer, windowbox plantings of busy lizzies, petunias, and lobelias become wonderfully full and luxuriant.*

FACING PAGE *Trailing geraniums in full bloom at the height of summer brighten up a plain window.*

HERB WINDOWBOX

You do not need even to own a garden to appreciate the pleasures of a windowsill lined with sun-loving herbs. Of all plants, aromatic herbs are particularly well-adapted to growing in a hot, dry position because this is not so different from the conditions they experienced on the rocky slopes above the Mediterranean, where so many of them had their origins. Growing herbs on a windowsill will also ensure that you can make the best possible use of the herbs because they will always be at hand whatever the weather.

WHILE MOST edible plants need to be grown in considerable quantities to supply enough food, even a small handful of freshly-picked herbs will turn a simple meal into a feast. A windowbox planted with sage (*Salvia officinalis*), lemon thyme (*Thymus × citriodorus*), rosemary (*Rosmarinus officinalis*), oregano (*Origanum*), and basil (*Ocimum basilicum*) will provide a full palette of flavors for your summer cookery.

When planting herbs as densely as this, it is advisable to choose a fairly deep container which will allow generous space for root growth and contain sufficient compost and nutrients to keep the herbs growing strongly all summer long. The addition of coarse grit to the compost will keep it free-draining, which is how most herbs prefer their soil.

One of the secrets of successful herb-growing is to keep picking the young stems regularly before they come into flower. This will ensure that the plants continue to make new growth and provide a steady supply of lush young shoots. With the exception of basil, all these herbs should survive the winter except in the coldest areas.

If you only have shady windowsills you can still grow herbs but you should choose those that do well in cooler conditions. Parsley (*Petroselinum crispum*), chervil (*Anthriscus cerefolium*), mint (*Mentha*) – a sprig of variegated mint is shown above – and sorrel (*Rumex*) are all suitable.

DISTRESSING A WINDOWBOX

There is now a very wide range of wood stains available for the garden which are preservative as well as colorful. The great advantage of these is that they are easy to apply because they are water-based, quick-drying and do not harm plants. This means that the maintenance and decoration of wooden windowboxes, tubs and planters has become much simpler. This windowbox has been given a distressed finish by first applying and rubbing down a coat of wood stain and then applying and rubbing down a coat of emulsion paint.

1 Paint the windowbox with bright blue wood stain. When dry, rub down lightly with fine sandpaper.

2 Apply a light coat of emulsion paint in a terracotta shade over the blue wood stain.

3 When dry, give the windowbox another rub down with sandpaper so that the blue and terracotta blend together to give a gently distressed finish. The windowbox can be sealed with matt varnish or left to weather gradually.

HERBS FOR THE DISTRESSED WINDOWBOX

ABOVE A windowbox filled with the herbs (left) is a sweetly scented addition to any kitchen. It is also much more convenient than having to go into the garden whenever you want to pick some herbs.

Oregano

(*Origanum*)

Lemon thyme

(*Thymus × citriodorus*)

Sage

(*Salvia officinalis*)

Basil

(*Ocimum basilicum*)

Painted Tins

Garden centers and nurseries make fortunes selling terracotta pots and fancy planters, but it isn't always necessary to spend a great deal of money to achieve stylish results. Using a coat of bright paint, you can transform empty tin cans into attractive and functional plant holders. Be very careful to make sure that the cut edges of the tin cans have been smoothed down or covered in masking tape to avoid accidents.

ALTHOUGH THERE is undoubtedly much to inspire us in the great gardens of the world there is also inspiration to be found in simple cottage gardens with their uncontrived planting and use of 'found' materials. Old car tires, leaky buckets, and enamel saucepans are all given a second lease of life as containers for plants and now that recycling has increasingly become part of our everyday lives, there is pleasure to be gained from transforming a humble tin can into something of enduring usefulness.

In a small garden, simple planters made from tin cans are a colorful and lightweight alternative to terracotta and can be used to adorn wall spaces, windowsills, and table tops. Filled with seasonal flowers which complement or contrast with the color of the painted tins, they will provide a year-round show. The tins make charming containers for cottage garden plants and can be used to great effect on windowsills to display supermarket herbs. In this case, you do not need to provide drainage holes – instead, fill the base of the tin with a layer of gravel to prevent the herbs becoming waterlogged.

ABOVE *For a cool look, plant the tin cans with white marguerites (Argyranthemum frutescens).*

RIGHT *Plant a selection of marigolds (Calendula) and lobelia – the orange and purple flowers contrast vividly with the bright blue paint of the tin cans. Double-flowered marigolds (top) can be used instead.*

TRANSFORMING TIN CANS

A touch of paint will transform a tin can into an elegant container. Family-sized tin cans will hold a 4in (10cm) flowerpot, but for larger plants you will need catering-sized tins. Ask your local pizza parlor or Italian restaurant for their empty tinned tomatoes cans – generally, they are happy to pass them on to you.

1 Use a sturdy nail and hammer to punch drainage holes in the base of the tin cans.

2 Most tin-openers leave a smooth cut edge, but if in doubt you should cover the edges of the tins with masking tape.

3 Paint the tins with a coat of gloss paint, being careful to cover any masking tape thoroughly. Leave to dry.

SEASONAL WINDOW DISPLAY

While most garden activities are curtailed or inhibited during the colder months of the year, the great advantage of windowbox gardening is that you don't even need to venture outdoors. Simply open your window and you are ready to plant, feed, and tend your mini-garden, and will enjoy an attractive and colorful display all year round.

Most of us will have enjoyed the pleasure of a summer windowbox with luxuriant flowers tumbling over the sills and delicious scents drifting indoors, but summer is the season of abundance when the windowbox must compete with many other contenders for your attention. The impact of the fall, winter, and early spring windowbox is quite different; these are times when our attention is generally focused inwards and gardening is not a daily activity, so there is a particular pleasure in looking through a window and seeing bright flowers before you notice the leafless trees, bare borders and gray skies beyond.

Some of the techniques for windowbox gardening are different in the cooler months. It is best not to use a compost with added moisture-retaining gel because this will tend to rot the roots – an ordinary, proprietary brand of potting compost used alone or mixed half-and-half with a soil-based compost will be better. Feeding is generally unnecessary and watering should only be done if the plants look very thirsty, and then only in frost-free conditions. What you can grow during the winter depends very

RIGHT *A spring display of dwarf narcissus and pansies in which the attractive scalloped form of the windowbox is clearly visible.*

COLOR-THEMED PLANTINGS

The following color-themed combinations would look good at different times of the year:

Winter display
Pink heathers (Erica gracilis) with pink cyclamens, pink winter-flowering pansies and variegated ivies.

Spring display
Muscari armeniacum, with blue pansies and polyanthus, and the same variegated ivies.

Summer display
Lobelia 'Sapphire', blue *Felicia amelloides* and deep-blue sage (*Salvia*) with thyme and ivies.

Fall display
Purple/blue ornamental cabbages with mauve winter-flowering pansies, dwarf cypresses and ivies.

much on the area in which you live; be guided by what your garden center recommends and accept that occasionally exceptionally cold weather will wreak havoc in such an exposed position.

Because most windowboxes are more or less at table-top level they are ideal for close-up viewing, so it is worth paying a little extra attention to detail. Choose compact varieties so they are less liable to wind damage, and look for plants that have interesting markings that will reward close inspection. Although you should not buy plants in flower in the summer, you can do so in the cooler months because the flowers last much longer at this time of year. After planting, cover the soil with moss or bark to conserve moisture.

LEFT *The window-box in its summer guise with mauve petunias and pansies, variegated coleus, and white and pink osteospermums.*

RIGHT *The winter display with cyclamens and variegated ivies.*

BALCONIES & PATIOS

If you live in a city, a balcony or terraced patio may be your entire garden, but limited space does not mean you need to limit your imagination. Your patio can be transformed into what appears to be a fragment of a much larger garden by using everything on a grand scale and including mirrors to create an

illusion of space. On a balcony, planting on several levels using wall pots, shelves, and columns, lets you fill your space with color and pay tribute to a dream garden.

ABOVE *A rustic wooden trough, filled with pink geraniums, links the veranda to the planting of pink busy lizzies (Impatiens) at its edge.*

RIGHT *A handsome marble slab on classical-style pillars is the ideal place for this similarly classical formal arrangement of ivy topiary frames and a trough of salvias.*

M OST BALCONY AND patio gardens consist almost entirely of container plants. The advantage of using containers is that you can treat the space like a stage set and move everything around without having to uproot your favorite plants. Plan major changes for the end of a season when you can assess the condition of the plants and trim, fertilize, or discard them as necessary. This is also an opportunity to sweep up dead leaves, dispose of any snails and slugs that you uncover, and generally give the whole area a facelift. Between the seasons, move smaller plants around to keep the view interesting. Container plants need regular watering and this can be very time-consuming, but there

BELOW *A balcony table in spring creates the perfect place for an informal display of flowering bulbs.*

are ways to make your task easier. Gravel-filled saucers under the pots will help retain moisture and groupi̶n̶g̶ ̶t̶o̶g̶ether cuts down on e̶v̶a̶p̶o̶r̶a̶ ̶

f̶i̶b̶e̶r̶g̶l̶a̶s̶s̶ ̶p̶o̶t̶s̶ ̶n̶e̶e̶d̶ ̶l̶ ̶ ̶t̶e̶r̶r̶a̶c̶o̶t̶t̶a̶ ̶o̶n̶e̶s̶ ̶a̶n̶d̶ ̶a̶r̶e̶ ̶m̶u̶c̶h̶ l̶i̶g̶h̶t̶e̶r̶,̶ ̶w̶h̶i̶c̶h̶ ̶c̶a̶n̶ ̶b̶e̶ ̶a̶n̶ ̶i̶m̶p̶o̶r̶t̶a̶n̶t̶ consideration on a balcony. If you don't l̶i̶k̶e̶ ̶t̶h̶e̶ ̶l̶o̶o̶k̶ ̶o̶f̶ ̶p̶l̶a̶s̶t̶ic flowerpots, slip them inside more decorative clay containe̶r̶s̶.

If you have to carry water from an indoor faucet, make the effort to fill the watering can again when you have finished – you can then use it on wilting plants in between your regular watering sessions. A balcony or patio with an outside faucet can make use of one of the automatic watering systems which are available from garden centers. A microchip-controlled timer is attached to the faucet and water is fed to each plant through a network of thin tubes. It sounds more complicated than it is, and once set up it will free you from the task of watering. All plants grown in containers will benefit from mulch, which retains moisture as well as provides extra nutrients.

ABOVE *On a curved terrace with wide walls, the planting follows the line of the architecture, with a seasonally changing display dominated, in spring, by containers of colorful tulips.*

RAISED POTS

For maximum impact and variety in a small area, it is essential to use the available vertical space wherever possible – not just on walls, but on any terraced areas and borders. Raising some pots above others creates a bank of color, rather than a flat plane, and allows the plants to be admired individually rather than en masse.

ALTHOUGH POTS come in many shapes and sizes, big pots are not always practical or affordable on a patio or balcony, and without a variation in size the pots can look rather uninspired, unless they are arranged at different levels. At its simplest, this can be done by placing one pot on another empty, upturned pot – this can be a useful function for a cracked or damaged pot.

Old architectural pots are a very attractive and reasonably inexpensive way to raise other pots and can be bought from junk yards or some garden centers. Invest in a few of varying heights and they will be in constant use as plinths for raised pots. The ornate ones can be very beautiful and expensive, but are more suitable as a focal point. The simple elegance of plain pots makes them better plinths. Topped with a terracotta or ceramic saucer, they will provide a stable base for a plant.

Metal stands have a simple, architectural beauty that is suitable for a formal area with topiary and evergreen planting. Although quite expensive to buy, they are a real asset to this style of gardening. If you can't find any at garden centers, an ironworker may be prepared to make them for you. An old-fashioned metal washstand is a ready-made alternative that would look wonderful in a more informal setting.

On the patio or balcony, where every inch of space is precious, the position-

ing of a plinth against tall-growing plants can give you an extra area of display between ground level and the flowers. Once you start "layering" the plants this way, you will realize the potential to add greater substance and interest to your gardening.

For those with a taste for the classical, pillars and columns make wonderful raised plant stands. They can be topped with large urns of handsome feature plants or softer displays of trailing plants, depending on the situation and the effect you want to create. If you do

ABOVE *Disused architectural pots make an attractive and effective way of raising plants, creating a tiered display of wallflowers, daffodils, euphorbia, dicentra, and forget-me-nots.*

LEFT AND TOP LEFT *Metal pot stands create an opportunity to raise plants off the balcony or patio floor. Trailing ivies are ideal for this situation.*

not have the budget for classical stone or marble pillars, try paint effects on plastic or fiberglass replicas. Seen from a distance, they can look deceptively like the real thing.

Whatever you use to raise the height of the display, you instantly create a 3-D effect, giving the space a greater depth than it would otherwise have, and increasing the apparent dimensions of the area. With clever use of raised containers, an almost jungle-like planting can deceive the eye into believing the garden is without boundaries.

ABOVE *Tiered plant displays at the edge of a patio, with metal pot stands and a rustic cane wigwam, help to mark the division between patio and garden. Raising small flowering bulbs, like tulips, to eye level increases their impact.*

LEFT *A cherub holds aloft a basket of double-flowered primroses on a patio wall.*

HOT COLORS

Until fairly recently it was fashionable in gardening to keep the palette restricted and to concentrate on cool, soft colors. Pretty as they are, they don't appeal to the more extrovert gardeners who like to make an impact with their plants and find the bright, hot colors much more appealing. Fortunately for them, in the same way that many of us are now using much stronger colors in our homes and manufacturers are meeting that need, so growers are also beginning to expand their range of vibrantly colorful plants to please even the most boldly extrovert gardener.

RIGHT *A vibrant display of azaleas and geraniums, on a low table and chair, provide a splash of strong color on a balcony.*

BALCONIES OR PATIOS are very restrictive areas in which to make a garden, and subtle planting can quickly become rather boring. A little like attractive but undemanding wallpaper, it is appreciated when first seen but soon goes unnoticed. Bright, hot colors grab the attention and cannot be ignored, especially when used in a small area. At its most basic, you can use a single color, even a single variety of plant that is massed for impact – little can rival the bright red of the geranium (*Pelargonium*) when it is in full bloom. But if even this is too subtle for you, choose the hot colors of India – orange marigolds (*Calendula officinalis*), purple heliotrope (*Heliotropium*), lime green tobacco plants (*Nicotiana*), magenta petunias (*Petunia*), shocking pink verbenas (*Verbena*), and scarlet geraniums. Planted separately in blocks of color, or massed together in a glorious hodge-podge, these plants will vibrate with color and may even cause more delicate souls to wince. To maintain the plants in prime condition, it is essential to water them daily, and a regular liquid fertilizer will help keep the flowers and foliage vibrant. Deadhead as often as you have time and cut back any stems that become leggy to encourage the growth of new foliage and flowers. With this sort of care, your balcony or patio will remain colorful from early summer right through to the fall.

FACING PAGE *A stone ledge creates a planting place for bright red geraniums.*

RIGHT *Clashing hot colors – of scarlet pelargoniums and brilliant blue lobelia, backed with hebes, provide an eye-catching display in this little alcove behind a balcony.*

EDIBLE DISPLAYS

Nothing ever tastes quite as good as home-grown food, and although the

small garden is unlikely to provide enough space for anyone other than the

dedicated enthusiast to grow serious amounts

of produce, it does add an extra, very

enjoyable, dimension to gardening.

Many edible plants can be

grown successfully in containers,

but it is sensible to stick to the more

decorative varieties of vegetable, which

will blend attractively with the rest of the

plants in the garden.

T HESE DAYS, garden centers have realized that many gardeners do not have the time, space, or inclination to grow fruit and vegetable plants from seed. As a result, they stock an ever-increasing range of compact varieties of plants ready for planting, from tomatoes (*Lycopersicon esculentum*), eggplants (*Solanum melongena*), and chilies (*Capsicum annuum*) to miniature fruit trees, all of which will perform well in pots. Look for the healthiest plants with strong stems and deep green coloring – lanky, pale plants that have been starved of food or water at this early stage will never grow well.

Try to be realistic in your choice of plants, even if you are tempted by all the varieties on offer. If your garden is in more or less permanent shade, you will never be able to grow tomatoes successfully, while alpine strawberries (*Fragaria vesca*) prefer shady corners to bright sunlight. As with all gardening, growing the right plant in the right place is ultimately far more rewarding than fighting the odds.

Edible plants are "gross feeders," which means they will need plenty of nutrients incorporated into the soil mix and regular liquid fertilizer throughout the growing season. A layer of composted humus in the base of the pot will provide a rich source of nourishment for mature plants, and pelleted manure added to the soil mix at the time of planting will ensure strong growth. If you add to this a weekly dose of a multipurpose liquid fertilizer, you will be sure to produce bumper crops.

ABOVE *A moss-lined wicker basket provides the ideal growing environment for alpine strawberries and makes a particularly attractive container for these pretty plants. Placed on a shady garden table, it is an eye-catching centerpiece.*

Pests find edible plants just as delicious as we do, so you will need to be vigilant. Top of the hit-list are slugs and snails, which can chomp their way through ripening fruit and vegetables at an alarming rate.

Slug pellets are an effective deterrent to these pests, and a wide band of petroleum jelly smeared around the pot, just below the rim, will also halt slugs in their tracks. Positioning any pots on sharp gravel is another effective slug deterrent.

STRAWBERRY BASKET

A basket planted up with alpine strawberries is easy to prepare and looks extremely decorative.

1 *Line the wicker basket with a generous layer of sphagnum moss to help retain moisture and prevent the soil from trickling out.*

2 *Fill the basket with soil and plant the strawberry plants firmly so that the soil is level with the base of the stems. Water well.*

ABOVE *Some varieties of cherry tomato are ideal for growing in pots. The bite-size fruit is both decorative and sweetly flavored.*

RIGHT *If your tomato plants grow abundantly, their stems will need support. Here, each stem has been tied to supporting canes, topped off with tiny terracotta pots.*

POND IN A POT

A pond is a desirable and attractive feature in any garden, but it can also be expensive to install when you take into account the cost of providing a water supply and power to the garden. This "pond in a pot" does away with the need for both these amenities, creating an instant "pond" for decorative water plants and even small fish.

IN THE COURTYARD gardens of China, beautiful glazed pots raised on plinths and planted with prize waterlilies (*Nymphaea*) are often a central feature. They allow you to truly admire the porcelain perfection of the blooms and, perhaps surprisingly, provide ideal conditions for the plants.

Waterlilies flower best when growing in deep, still water in full sun and, when given these conditions, will send up a succession of flowers over many months. During the first year the plant will be establishing itself and may not flower, so the addition of some marginal water plants will add interest to the pond. Unlike waterlilies, marginal plants do not like to be planted deep, preferring to have their roots in the water and their leaves in the air. By forming a ledge on one side of the pot you can create an ideal habitat for these plants. Once planted and filled with water, the pot will quickly create a balanced environment and the only care it will need is occasionally filling up with water and the removal of algae, which forms in the presence of light. The easiest way to do this is to poke a garden cane into the center of the mass of algae and twist it so the weed wraps itself around the cane and can be removed.

Warning This pond is not recommended in a garden used by small children. The safe alternative is a pot filled with river stones and marginal plants growing among the stones.

OPPOSITE *This pond provides a tranquil focal point in a small courtyard and needs no more attention than occasionally filling up with water from a hose.*

PREPARING A POND IN A POT

For your pond you will need a large, glazed, frost-proof pot. The glaze is essential or the water will quickly evaporate through the terracotta. Fortunately, many of these pots are now imported from China and other Asian countries and are relatively inexpensive. Most large pots will have drainage holes in the base, but these are easily sealed with epoxy putty, which is available from hardware stores and from some art-and-craft suppliers. Follow the manufacturer's instructions for use.

1 *Once the drainage holes are sealed, cover the base of the pot with a layer of washed stones. Any soil that settles in the base of the pot will remain undisturbed under the stones.*

2 *Plant the waterlily in an aquatic basket lined with burlap and filled with a specially formulated aquatic soil mix. All of these will be available where you buy the waterlily.*

3 *Place the lily basket to one side in the base of the pot. When it is in position, cover the surface of the soil surrounding the lily with more stones.*

4 *Move the pot to its chosen position in the garden. Use a couple of bricks or large stones to create a ledge inside the pot next to the lily basket and position your marginal plants. Gently fill the pot with water using a hose. Let it to overflow to remove any debris from the surface. The pond will be cloudy for a few days until it settles down.*

GARDENING BASICS

You need very little gardening knowledge to create successful plantings for small spaces: there are a wide range of container-grown plants you can buy and, provided you follow the instructions on the labels, they should be easy to maintain. If you wish to save yourself money, it pays to have some basic information about choosing plants and keeping them in good condition, and perhaps, even more importantly, which plants you can raise yourself from seed or cuttings.

ABOVE *Simple containers can be painted to give them a more attractive appearance. This little metal pot has been given a verdigris finish.*

RIGHT *A dedicated work space makes simple garden tasks easier to perform, ideally with storage under or above for equipment and containers.*

TOOLS & CONTAINERS

The basic tools you need to begin are shown below, and you can add to these as your experience grows, including specialized equipment if, for example, you wish to grow plants from seed and decide that a propagation unit is worthwhile. Containers are available in all sizes and materials, a range of which is shown right.

TOOLS

Try to find a suitable place to keep your equipment, preferably somewhere dry and airy so the tools will not get damp and rust, and with a workbench where you can carry out simple gardening jobs. A garden notebook is invaluable. If you can teach yourself to write down what you have bought, and where you put it, you will save yourself many headaches wondering what happened to the crocuses, or where you put the cyclamen corms!

Basic Cultivating Tools

There are four essential items for a basic tool kit: a garden trowel; a hand fork; pruners; and a knife.

Pruners

Knife

Trowel

Hand fork

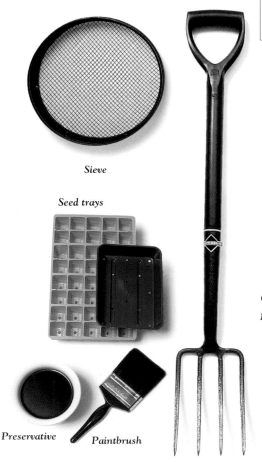

Sieve

Seed trays

Preservative *Paintbrush*

Fork

Hose (not essential but very useful)

Canes and ties for staking

Fine-spray nozzle

Watering can

Pest Control

Insecticidal sprays can be used to control flying insects; slug pellets destroy slugs and snails.

Hand-held sprayer

Slug pellets

TYPES OF CONTAINER

Containers are made from many materials, some more expensive than others, so much depends on what you can afford and the purpose and position of the container. If you want to create a focal point with an urn on a pedestal, for example, you may want to splurge on a quality stone or terracotta container, but if you want to create an informal windowsill display, you could just recycle household tin cans, painting them a strong color (see below).

Terracotta ▲

One of the oldest and most traditional materials, terracotta weathers attractively, is not too expensive, and suits most plants. It is heavy, can shatter in cold conditions, and breaks easily if knocked over.

Natural stone ▲

Durable and permanent, stone can be carved into handsome shapes. It is expensive, as well as extremely heavy.

Wire ▶

Containers of galvanized wire add a baroque touch to the garden. They are light and attractive.

▲ Plastic and fiberglass

Lightweight, durable, and portable, these materials are unattractive to look at, but can be hand-painted and distressed to give a much more natural appearance.

◀ Wood

Softwood is relatively cheap but needs preserving and painting or it will rot very quickly. It is quite heavy, so should be used with care on balconies and roof gardens where the additional weight may be a problem.

Cement ▲

Although much cheaper than natural stone, cement does not have the same natural beauty. It can, however, be molded into various shapes.

LEFT Former catering-size tomato cans have been painted bright blue and filled with colorful summer flowers.

GETTING STARTED

Before you stock your garden with plants, check that you have

at least the basic equipment needed to maintain your

garden properly. Make sure that any

containers for the plants look attractive –

they are, after all, a major part of the display

in a small space.

Y**OU CAN BUY** almost any plant you desire these days, ready to plant out in its own container. What determines the cost of the plant is its size – the longer it has been looked after in the nursery, the more expensive it will be. You will have to balance out the relative merits and disadvantages of each. You will get more young plants for your money, and they will establish themselves well and quickly, but they will take longer to fill the space allocated for them. Mature plants will do this more successfully, but will be slower to establish themselves and will cost you a great deal more. Plants can be bought from mail-order catalogs, direct from specialist suppliers and nurseries, or from garden centers. A lot depends on where you are living, and the kind of plants you wish to purchase. Garden centers usually carry a good range of popular perennials, shrubs, and trees, but specialist growers tend to stock more unusual species and varieties of plant, which may be of greater interest if you wish to develop a collection of one particular type of plant, for example. Some garden centers look after their plants better than others, and the signs of a well-run plant nursery include clear labeling, weed-free, moist soil, and no obvious symptoms of diseases in the plants themselves. You can also grow your own plants from seed, or from bulbs or cuttings (see pages 112-3).

RULES FOR CHOOSING PLANTS

• Check that the plant is not crowded in its container.
• Avoid plants where the soil at the top of the pot is weedy and mossy – the plant has been neglected.
• Pick a plant with a well-formed shape – no long, straggly shoots.
• Make sure the leaves are strong and healthy – check the undersides for signs of disease, such as whitefly.
• Avoid plants in full flower, as they stand up less well to transportation.
• If the plant looks at all unwell, check that its roots are not growing out through the holes in the base of the container. If they are, the plant is probably pot-bound; that is, it has grown too big for its pot.

Plant Size
The larger the plant, the more expensive it will be, but the quicker it will fill the available space. Use small plants for group planting schemes, and buy large specimens for feature spots.

Mature
Skimmia japonica

Immature
Skimmia japonica

It is vital that the plant's roots are not restricted, as these take up food and water.

Potting Soil

If you garden in a city on a window-box, balcony, or roof garden, you will need enough soil mix (a mixture of soil and nutrients and minerals) to fill any containers you plant. The larger the bag, the cheaper, but large bags are very difficult to handle, particularly up flights of stairs, so you may find it more practical to opt for more, smaller bags.

You will need at least two kinds of soil: one for general planting and another for propagating plants (the former being a richer mixture). You can also get specially prepared growing medium for specific types of plant: for example, rhododendrons and camellias need acid soil, and require a specially acid soil mix. Peat-free soil mixes are considered more environmentally friendly than those which contain peat.

Container Plants

Most plant purchases these days are of container-grown plants that you just remove from their plastic flowerpot and repot into your own container. Plants are supplied in other forms, most notably trees, which are often mailed as bare-root specimens. Being woody and fairly tough, they will survive for a short time without a growing medium around their roots.

A container-grown palm comes in its own plastic pot; it must be removed and replanted in a larger pot or in the ground.

When trees and shrubs are supplied as bare-root plants, without a pot, their roots need a good soaking in a bucket of water before planting.

Planting

How you plant depends, to a large extent, on what kind of plant you are growing, and what sort of root system it has. As a beginner's guide, the roots must be covered with soil and the stem exposed to the elements. In general, any container must be about 4in (10cm) larger than the plant in diameter. If it is bigger or smaller than that, the plant will not establish so readily. Any planting hole you make in a bed must be large enough for the plant's roots to be able to spread out properly. Repotting is really the same exercise, but involves transferring the plant to a larger pot with new potting soil – a job carried out, for most plants, every couple of years when the plant outgrows its existing pot. If the roots start to come out of the base of the pot, you should repot anyway. Do not choose a pot that is much larger than the original, since this may cause root problems. Basically, you need a new pot that is just big enough for a layer of new soil to fit around the existing root ball. Before transplanting, let the plant dry out slightly, so that the root ball slides out of the old pot easily and is not damaged in the process.

Bulbs

Bulbs are generally planted several months before they flower, so spring-flowering bulbs are normally planted in early and mid-fall. Summer-flowering bulbs, such as the big regale lilies, are usually planted in early spring. The depth at which they are planted depends on the size of the bulb, but as a rule, plant bulbs at twice the depth of the bulb itself. When flowering is over, move the container of bulbs to a more out-of-the-way place, and keep the pot watered to provide food for next year's flowers.

1 Hold the plant by the stem, turn the pot upside down, and ease the plant from its old pot. Fill the new pot with a drainage layer and some fresh soil.

2 Carefully insert the plant into its new pot, filling any spaces with fresh potting soil. Firm it gently, then water the plant and leave to drain.

Such bulbs as lilies produce scales that can be separated from the parent in fall. Seal these in a plastic bag with peat and fungicide and leave in the dark for 12-14 weeks. Tiny white bulblets will form at the base of each scale, which can then be potted.

FERTILIZERS & WATER

Regular fertilizing and watering are essential to the wellbeing of any plant, but especially so for plants in containers, which can dry out and lose nutrients very quickly. To keep plants strong and healthy, there are various forms of fertilizer available that can be added to the soil to release nutrients gradually throughout the growing season, or given as a quick boost. Water should be applied frequently, keeping in mind that a little often is better than an occasional drowning.

FERTILIZERS

Plants will not survive very long in limited growing conditions without regular applications of fertilizer, which is available in a variety of forms.

Slow-release granules can be added to the soil mix at planting time and will release nutrients gradually and regularly throughout the growing season. They depend on moisture to work, so make sure the soil does not dry out.

Liquid fertilizers are normally given weekly in the growing season. They are diluted with water according to the manufacturer's instructions, and then watered onto the soil. Most liquid fertilizers are multipurpose, but you can also buy or make up specialized ones. For example, certain formulas can give a quick boost to promote flowering or fruiting.

Dry fertilizer can be added to the soil mix at the time of planting to provide long-term nutrition, or added to a border or bed after planting, but take care that it does not touch flower stems. Rain or hose-watering will then soak the fertilizer into the soil.

Using Dry Fertilizers

Sprinkle dry fertilizer evenly over the soil and then mix into the top layer with a fork or trowel. If the soil is dry, water after applying the fertilizer because this will help dissolve it and wash it down toward the roots.

WATER

Containers, in particular, dry out very fast and the main labor in any small garden well-furnished with containers or hanging baskets is regular watering. In hot weather, hanging baskets may need watering twice a day. Try not to water in full sunlight, because water splashed directly onto leaves in hot sun will cause scorching.

1 *Make a few small holes with a pencil around the rim of the pot to provide a conduit for the water so it reaches the roots.*

Using Liquid Fertilizers

1 *Dilute liquid fertilizers with water according to the manufacturer's instructions, and mix thoroughly to reduce the chance of damaging the plants.*

2 *Apply the fertilizer directly to the soil around the base of the plant, or as a foliar feed. Either way, nutrients will reach the plant very quickly.*

2 *Give an adequate quantity of water to each plant, so the soil at the base is as moist as the soil on the surface.*

Reviving a Wilted Plant

Smaller quantities of water at regular intervals are better for plants than infrequent soakings, which simply raise their stress levels, making them more prone to disease. If a plant has wilted, you may be able to revive it by placing it in a bucket of water for 10 minutes. When bubbles cease to rise to the surface, the soil is soaked.

Vacation Watering

When you go away, you will need to make provision for your plants to be watered. For short-term vacation care, wick watering or capillary matting feeds water to plants via the wick or matting material from a reservoir. To help reduce evaporation in the height of summer, place the containers together on a tray of pebbles. Small plants, in particular, will benefit from this and will draw up moisture from the tray, by capillary action. In very hot weather, water the patio as well – the wet stone will help to cool down the area, reducing evaporation from the containers.

ABOVE *When you go away, place pot plants on a tray of pebbles in water. Take hanging baskets down (right), stand them on buckets in shady positions, and water well. Ask a friend to water twice a week.*

RIGHT *Hanging baskets and wall pots can be watered more easily using a hose with a cane attached to the last yard length of the hose to create a "rigid" spout.*

Watering Hanging Baskets

Hanging baskets need copious amounts of water in summer. Being exposed to the elements on all sides, with only a thin protective covering of moss or liner for the soil, they dry out extremely quickly.

Hanging baskets can be suspended on a pulley system for ease of watering. If not, you need to construct a spout for a hose (see right). It cuts down on watering time if you include water-retaining crystals in the soil mix before you plant.

RIGHT *Scattering water-retaining crystals in the soil of a hanging basket will ensure that the plants do not dry out rapidly.*

PROPAGATING

Plants can be propagated (increased) in various ways,

the easiest methods being from seed or from parts cut

off the plant (cuttings) which are then inserted directly

into potting soil so that roots form on the cut base, creating

a new plant.

GROWING FROM SEED

This method is ideal for colorful annuals, where quite a few are needed, but not worth the bother for just a couple of plants. The majority of seed packets contain hundreds of seeds, and it is hardly economical in this case. Many seeds need fairly warm conditions to germinate, and once planted, are usually put in a light, warm (but not hot or sunny) place to germinate (sprout). They will not do so without an adequate supply of moisture, the amount of which needs to be carefully regulated. A plastic bag over a watered seed tray will usually provide ideal germination conditions. When the seedlings are large enough to handle, they can then be transplanted into small individual pots, and repotted again when they are large enough to be put outside.

Collecting Seed

Choose the strongest, healthiest plants from which to collect seed, because this will ensure the best chance of successful propagation. Poor plants provide inferior material, and their seeds are much less likely to grow into robust new plants. Timing is also vital when collecting seeds – if you gather them too early, they will not germinate, too late and the seeds will already have been dispersed.

Thoroughly dry seedheads can be hung up in a plastic bag to collect seeds.

1 *Prepare a tray of seed soil mix. Sieve the soil if necessary to remove any large lumps. Moisten thoroughly.*

2 *Sow the seed at the required depth – the smaller the seed, the shallower the depth. For fine seed, sow in a long drill. For larger seeds (such as sweet peas), sow individually.*

3 *Water with a fine-spray nozzle on the watering can. Cover with plastic and leave in a light, warm, but not hot, place until germination occurs.*

Sowing large seeds

Leaving space between the top of the soil and the pot rim, sow seeds on the surface. If the seed needs darkness to germinate, cover with a layer of soil. Water the pot from below and cover it with a piece of glass.

Seedheads of poppies, shaken onto brown paper, for collection and future use.

Sowing Seeds Successfully

- Use a good quality soil mix.
- Use clean pots and trays.
- Remember that seeds need an initial period of darkness.
- Once germinated, seeds must have light. Turn the tray around regularly to ensure an even distribution.
- Seed soil mixes contain only enough nutrients for 6 weeks, so repot after that.
- Seedlings must not dry out. Regular, gentle watering works best.
- Thin out ruthlessly to ensure seedlings are sturdy. Plant 25 percent more seeds than you need to make up for fatalities.
- Harden off seedlings grown indoors before planting them outside by exposing them to outdoor conditions in daylight for 10 days or so.

▲ *Putting seeds or cuttings in a heated propagator speeds up rooting and germinating.*

A cold frame is used ▶ *to gradually acclimatize seedlings to the outdoor conditions before planting them.*

GROWING FROM CUTTINGS

One advantage of growing plants from cuttings, as opposed to seed, is that you know exactly what plant you will get. Generally, shrubs are grown from cuttings and annuals and most perennials from seed.

Cuttings can be taken from all parts of the plant – stems, shoots, buds, leaves, and even roots – and the method differs according to which part you are using. The most commonly used type of cutting is known as the softwood cutting (shown right), which is taken from a young shoot in summer. It is relatively easy to persuade a softwood cutting to root, but some plants will root more easily than others. Good candidates for this purpose are boxwood (*Buxus sempervirens*) and geraniums. Cuttings are usually taken in early or midsummer from a nonflowering shoot and will be ready to transfer into individual pots in the fall. To take cuttings, you will need a 6in (15cm) diameter pot, filled with a cuttings soil mix, and a sharp knife. Root-inducing hormone can be applied to the base of the cutting to encourage rooting. It is important to use the right mixture of soil for cuttings. Usually a mixture of three parts sand and one part soil is used, because it gives the necessary drainage for the plant, which in turn prevents rotting. Cuttings must be kept moist in good light but out of direct sun.

1 *Carefully remove a young shoot from the parent plant (pelargonium) that has three or four leaves on it.*

2 *Remove the bottom pair of leaves, clearing the lower half of the stem so it is able to be inserted into the soil medium.*

3 *Dip the base of the cutting in root-inducing hormone. With a pencil or dibble, make a small hole in the soil to take the cutting. Insert the cutting.*

4 *Firm soil around the cutting, water well, and keep the soil moist until the new plant starts to grow. Place a clear plastic bag over the pot to form a mini greenhouse.*

113

MAINTAINING YOUR PLANTS

Your plants will need a certain amount of care to look good at all times. The important jobs, apart from applying fertilizer and water (see pages 110-1), are to stake and support them properly, and to remove any dead or dying flowers, as well as straggly growth or dying or damaged stems. Check regularly for pests and diseases, since all plant problems are easiest to deal with early on.

STAKING

Many plants, particulary soft-stemmed herbaceous perennials, need some kind of additional support to look good. There are many ways to create efficient and attractive staking systems for plants, and stakes or canes can be bought at garden centers (see below). Be careful, when tying plant stems to a stake, not to twist the tie so tight that it damages the stem. Softer, wider ties are better than string, which can cut through weak stems.

Forms of Staking

Link stakes

Fan trellis

Canes

Supporting Plants

With container plants, or plants in small gardens, the stake should be as invisible as possible. Alternatively, it can be sufficiently attractive – such as a neat cage of pussy willow twigs to support hyacinths, or a little fence of bamboo canes to support narcissi – to justify being displayed. Plants such as the big regale lilies, with heavy flowering heads, will have to be supported or they will droop or snap off. Equally, very spreading plants with soft stems, such as begonias and some geraniums, may need a gentle, unobtrusive helping hand to create a more attractive form for the plant. Wall shrubs and climbers will need tying onto a supporting structure, such as trellis or wires stretched across a wall or fence and attached with screw eyes.

Young shrubs with undeveloped stems are often supported with a garden stake, to which the plant is tied. Use soft plastic ties, and make sure that they are not too tight.

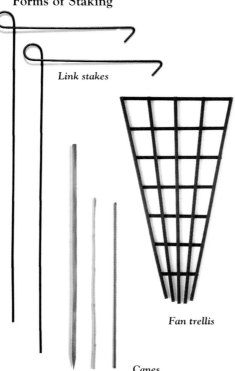

A simple system of canes, pushed into the soil mix or ground, and fastened with wire or string, can keep unruly plants in place.

A neat hoop made of linked metal stakes is useful for preventing soft-stemmed perennials from flopping over and getting damaged.

PRUNING

Most people become anxious at the prospect of pruning their plants, confused by a plethora of apparently conflicting advice and unclear instructions. There are two chief principles for pruning: one is to prune a woody-stemmed plant to improve its overall shape; the other is to prune it to increase the number of flowering shoots, and its consequent "flower power."

Before you become hopelessly confused, most plants will survive without pruning, but they will produce fewer and smaller flowers, their branches may start to cross over and tangle, and their overall appearance will be less attractive. Remember that the first requirement is to prune for health (by maintaining a good open shape) and the second for beauty (to get the most flowers). A few plants (*Buddlejas*, for example) do better when pruned very hard, but for most plants you should aim to remove about a third of the new growth each year. With overgrown roses, cut out a third of old stems at base level, to allow new stems to flourish.

Lopsided stems
To maintain the framework of the plant, cut back over-vigorous shoots lightly. Do not prune too hard, since this will stimulate growth.

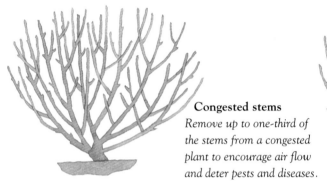

Congested stems
Remove up to one-third of the stems from a congested plant to encourage air flow and deter pests and diseases.

Weak stems
Cut out any weak, straggly stems because these are more vulnerable to pests and diseases.

Pruning for Shape

This kind of pruning is to prevent plants becoming straggly or "awkward" shapes. You can encourage the direction a branch takes by pruning back to a bud that is pointing in the direction you want the shoot to grow. This will help "open out" the center of the plant, encouraging the air to circulate, and the plant will be healthier and look better. Remove any diseased or damaged wood at the same time. Generally speaking, this kind of pruning is best done in the fall.

Pruning for Flowers

Shrubs and climbers flower at different times of the year, some of them on old wood (on flowering shoots rising from the main woody stems) and some on new wood (flowering shoots on sideshoots formed the previous year). Your pruning strategy depends on your knowing which you are dealing with!

Generally, spring-flowering shrubs and climbers flower on wood formed the previous season. Prune them once flowering stops by cutting the shoots that bore flowers back to two buds away from the main stem. If you prune these plants in spring, you will not get flowers, since you will be cutting off the shoots that flower! Late summer-flowering shrubs can also be cut back after flowering in fall, but could be pruned instead in spring (there will be time for new growth to form and flower). Some plants, such as clematis, have a range of flowering times depending on the species. To prune correctly, establish whether they are spring- or summer-flowering, then prune as above.

Light pruning only is all that is necessary for most evergreens, to improve the overall shape of the plant.

Pinching Out

You can encourage young plants to become more bushy if you stop the growth in the first year by removing the growing point (the leading shoot or shoots) of each plant. This encourages sideshoots to form, increasing the lateral spread of the plant. Remove the tip by pinching it out between finger and thumb, or with a sharp knife.

This technique is particularly valuable with plants such as boxwood, garniums, browallia, some petunias, and antirrhinums.

GARDEN JOBS

In addition to creating attractive plant groupings, you will

also need to carry out certain jobs to do with the hardware of

the garden: for example, attaching hooks or brackets for

hanging baskets and wall pots, repairing cracked or broken

containers, putting up trellis, and moving heavy containers.

REPAIRING POTS

If a terracotta pot shatters and it has broken cleanly, you can wire it under the rim of the pot. Place the pot upside down with the broken edges together. Cut a length of galvanized wire, about 10in (25cm) longer than the circumference of the pot. Ask an assistant to hold the wire tight around the pot rim, while you twist the ends to form a collar. Use a screwdriver blade to tighten the collar by rotating the blade. Trim with wire cutters.

To treat more complex breaks, use epoxy putty. Mix the two materials of the epoxy putty together as instructed by the manufacturer. Work the putty into a pliable strip. Dip the pieces of terracotta pot to be joined in water. Break off a piece of putty and roll it into a long, thin "snake." Press the putty to one broken edge, and position the matching broken piece on top of it. Push together to squeeze the putty into all the crevices. Trim off excess putty and leave overnight to set. Treat additional breaks in the same way, leaving to harden in between treatments.

Wet the edges of the broken pot. Using a palette knife, apply epoxy putty to all broken surfaces. Press together and tape the pot to keep the pieces in place. Remove when dry.

PAINTING POTS

Pots can be painted easily with modern acrylic paints and need little or no priming. Water-based paints are easy to use, look good, and can be repainted after a couple of years. A little weathering, however, often adds to the attraction. To paint a pot with a water-based latex paint, you will need to apply both a prime coat and an acrylic varnish.

1 *Paint the pot using the acrylic primer. This provides a seal for the pot's surface and a surface to act as a key for the paint.*

2 *Then paint the pot with latex paint, using first one coat, and then a second when the first one dries, if needed.*

3 *Finally, apply a coat of acrylic varnish and allow to dry.*

DECORATIVE PAINT EFFECTS

Pots of all kinds can benefit from attractive decoration, and these decorations can be as simple or as elaborate as your skills and taste allow. Plain terracotta pots look pretty with a decorated, painted rim, which is remarkably easy to create.

Alternatively, you could create a range of interesting paint effects on your pots, from crackle glaze, where the pot's surface acquires a wonderfully "aged" appearance, to sponging, where a runny, wet painted surface is worked into with a natural sponge, or even colorwashing, where a thin layer of paint is applied that allows the textured base surface to show through.

Painting a border

1 Make a template from heavyweight paper, using a coin as a guide for a semicircle design. Tape it to the rim.

2 Using a soft stippling brush, paint the rim of the pot, with a quick-drying acrylic paint.

3 When dry, you can remove the template to reveal a prettily decorated painted rim.

The finished decorated pot.

Ageing a Pot

Plain mass-produced terracotta pots look much prettier when they have weathered from a few seasons out of doors. This natural process can be speeded up using a coat of live yogurt.

1 Apply yogurt to the pot with a paintbrush. Place the pot out-of-doors to dry.

2 When the pot looks aged, and the yogurt has dried (after a few days), plant the pot in the usual way.

Attaching Hanging Baskets

Hanging baskets can be suspended from overhead swivel hooks or wall-mounted brackets. The swivel hook is usually attached to a metal plate, which is screwed to the underside of secure wood. The center of the metal plate is threaded to take the hook, which is screwed through the plate into the wooden support. If you want to raise and lower the hanging basket, you will need to attach a guide for a pulley to the metal plate, with a hook on the end of the pulley for the basket.

Supporting wall brackets

Wall brackets are generally made of wrought iron, and the length of the arm needs to be at least as long as half the diameter of the basket. The bracket will need to be screwed to a solid support, such as a wall or a secure wooden beam. Remember that the basket is extremely heavy when filled with saturated soil, so make sure the support for the bracket is solid enough to hold its weight.

Attaching windowboxes

Windowboxes on upper story windows need either a guard rail around the box or should be secured by chains to the wall, to prevent accidents. If your windows open outward, you need to secure the

A wire basket, filled with pansies, is suspended from a sturdy metal bracket.

windowbox to the wall using supporting brackets and similar retaining chains.

Securing safety chains

Drill holes in the masonry on the outside house wall about 12in (30cm) up from the base of the window, and about 3in (8cm) outside the window frame. Screw strong steel hooks into the holes. Screw in heavy-duty screw eyes to each end of the windowbox itself, at the outward facing end. Attach the windowbox to the wall using steel chain.

PLANT FINDER

Finding the right plant for the right place is the key to successful planting schemes. This section categorizes the most valuable plants into groups of most benefit to small-space gardeners. Anyone creating a planting scheme for a small space needs to look for a variety of plant forms, from small trees, climbers, and

shrubs, to tiny alpine plants, depending on the setting. They also need to ensure that the chosen plants will do well in the situation, since they all have different requirements.

ABOVE *Delicate flowers, like those of* Primula sieboldii, *should be planted where they can be seen in close-up to appreciate their fragile beauty.*

RIGHT *The silvery felted leaves of* Helichrysum petiolare *'Silverlight' with its trailing habit make an excellent addition to any hanging container.*

CLIMBERS & WALL SHRUBS

Rosa 'Variegata di Bologna'

Most small gardens have a wall or fence, or even a balcony rail, which will provide the support necessary for an interesting variety of climbers. Climbers are useful because they will scramble up or around any support using hooks, in the case of roses for example, twining tendrils or leafstalks, or twining stems. There is no shortage of climbers to choose from, many of them with abundant flowers in spring, summer, or fall, but the situation you have in mind should govern your choice, since some do better in shade or sun, and some in cool or hot situations.

For shady walls, the climbing hydrangea (*Hydrangea petiolaris*) or ivy (*Hedera helix*) are invaluable. For a sheltered wall, grow camellias with their glossy green leaves and marvelous oriental flowers in early spring. Sweet peas provide a short-lived but glorious display of scented flowers in full sun in summer, as do many of the climbing roses, some jasmines, and of course the ubiquitous honeysuckle, of which there are many varieties to choose from, some more glamorous in flower form, others more highly scented. A few honeysuckles will also do well in partial shade, such as *Lonicera periclymenum* and *L. × americana*.

Clematis is universally popular, with its varied flower forms from the tiny macropetala clematis to the saucer-size hybrids, and a species can be found to flower in most months of the year. They need a shaded root run and well-drained soil to survive. More vigorous species, such as *C. montana*, will need occasional pruning to keep them under control.

Wall shrubs differ from climbers in having no actual means of supporting themselves, and they will need to be tied to a framework of wires or trellis to keep them close to the supporting wall.

Camellia
Theaceae

H 3 – 12ft (1 – 4m)
S 2 – 6ft (0.6 – 1.8m)

Beautiful, glossy-leaved shrubs which prefer a lime-free soil mix, and are ideal in containers. Although they grow well in the open, they enjoy the shelter and warmth of a wall (not east-facing, as early sun spoils frosted blooms). *C. japonica* covers a huge range of hybrids, with single, semidouble, and double flowers in shades of red, pink, and white.

Clematis
OLD MAN'S BEARD
Ranunculaceae

H 6 – 46ft (1.8 – 14m)
S 2 – 6ft (0.6 – 1.8m)

The huge range of clematis available means that there is a variety in flower during every month of the year. Many will ramble through other plants without causing damage, adding an extra dimension to them. Creamy-flowered, evergreen *C. cirrhosa balearica* flowers in winter, the exuberant white- or pink-flowered *C. montana* and mauve-blue *C. macropetala* in spring, and the yellow *C. tangutica* in fall. Most of the large-flowered hybrids flower in summer. Among the most spectacular are *C.* 'Nelly Moser,' with pink-striped flowers; *C.* 'Ville de Lyon', with magenta flowers; and *C.* 'The President,' with purple flowers.

Convolvulus
BINDWEED
Convolvulaceae

H 12 – 24in (30 – 60cm)
S 16in (40cm) or more

C. althaeoides is a hardy, vigorous twining climber, bearing pink, funnel-shaped flowers. Its spread can be restricted by planting it in a container. *C. tricolor* has tall-growing forms with royal blue flowers, with yellow and white

centers. Blooms continuously in the summer; each flower lasts only a day. Frost-tender, needing a sunny, well-drained site.

Garrya elliptica
SILK TASSEL BUSH
Garryaceae

H and **S** 12ft (4m)

An upright, evergreen bush with glossy, wavy-edged leaves, grown for its winter display of long, gray-green male catkins. *G.e.* 'James Roof' has clusters of silvery catkins up to 8in (20cm) long. *G.e.* 'Evie' has catkins up to 12in (30cm) long. When trained against a wall, other plants, such as clematis, can be grown through it to give color in summer.

Hedera helix 'Glacier'
IVY
Araliaceae

H 6ft (1.8m) or more

Many of the ivies are suitable for growing against a wall, because they are tolerant of a wide range of conditions, and will support themselves as they become established. *H. h.* 'Glacier' has small, almost triangular-shaped leaves, which are variegated gray-green and cream. It is useful for covering a dull wall, wooden post, or fence, and it can also be grown as ground cover or as a houseplant.

Hydrangea petiolaris
CLIMBING HYDRANGEA
Hydrangeaceae

H 30ft (10m)

A deciduous, woody climber, which supports itself against a wall or fence as it grows by means of aerial roots. It has flattened white flowerheads in summer, consisting of both fertile and sterile florets. The long, heart-shaped leaves are dark green, turning golden-yellow in fall. It prefers moist soil and shelter from cold winds, but is fully hardy and tolerant of shade.

Jasminum
JASMINE
Oleaceae
H and **s** 10ft (3m)

J. nudiflorum (winter jasmine) is a floppy, deciduous shrub producing masses of fragrant, golden-yellow flowers in winter. It needs tying to its support, but will soon cover the lower part of a wall. *J. humile* bears bright yellow, sometimes scented, flowers from late spring to early fall. *J. officinale* (common jasmine) is a twining, deciduous climber, which produces clusters of highly scented white flowers in summer. All prefer full sun or partial shade and a moist soil.

Lathyrus odoratus
SWEET PEA
Leguminosae
H 2 – 8ft (0.6 – 2.5m)
s 18in (45cm)

Many cultivars and hybrids have been developed from these annual climbers with their distinctive scent. They climb, by means of tendrils, against walls and fences, or over other plants, preferring full sun and a fertile soil mix. Flower colors include red, salmon, pink, purple, violet, and white, in solid colors, shades or picotee (i.e. darker edging). Excellent as cut flowers.

Lonicera periclymenum
EARLY DUTCH
HONEYSUCKLE
Caprifoliaceae
H up to 22 ft (7m)

A vigorous climber with twining, woody stems, which need supporting against a wall, but will twist around trellis or the stems of other plants. This is one of the first honeysuckles to flower (mid-spring to midsummer). It produces tubular white flowers that age to yellow, with a red reverse to the petals. Likes a well-drained soil and full sun or partial shade. *L.p.* 'Serotina,' or Late Dutch honeysuckle, has creamy white flowers streaked with dark red-purple.

Parthenocissus tricuspidata
BOSTON IVY
Vitaceae
H 30ft (10m)

This is a vigorous, woody climber, which supports itself by means of tiny suckers at the tips of the tendrils. Its leaves are three-lobed and bright green, turning fiery-red to purple in fall. *P.t.* 'Beverley Brook' has purple-green foliage, turning bright red in fall. *P.t.* 'Veitchii' has purple-red fall colors. Tolerates sun or shade in a well-drained soil.

Pyracantha
FIRETHORN
Rosaceae
H and **s** 10ft (3m)

Tolerant, spiny, evergreen shrub with mid- to dark-green leaves and white flowers in spring, followed by berries in fall. Berry color varies: those of *P.* 'Mohave' are red-orange; *P.* 'Shawnee' are orange-yellow; *P.* 'Soleil d'Or' are golden-yellow; and *P.* × *watereri* are red.

Prunes back well against a wall or fence, and supports other climbers grown through it.

Rosa
ROSE
Rosaceae
H 10ft (3m) **s** 8ft (2.5m)

Climbing roses have vigorous, stiff stems with glossy foliage. Some flower once in summer, others repeatedly. *R.* 'New Dawn' has repeat, double flowers of pale pink. *R.* 'Maigold' has semidouble yellow flowers in one main flush, followed by a sparse second. *R.* 'Mme Alfred Carrière' has double pale-pink to white flowers from summer to fall. (See also page 133, SEASONAL COLOR: SUMMER).

Solanum crispum
CHILEAN POTATO TREE
Solanaceae
H 10ft (3m) **s** 6ft (1.8m)

A scrambling evergreen or semi-evergreen climber, which needs supporting against a wall or fence. It has dark green leaves and fragrant purple flowers in clusters at the end of the stems, followed by pale yellow fruit. *S.c.* 'Glasnevin' has dark purple-blue flowers from summer to fall. Grow in full sun, and protect the plant in winter, since it is not frost-hardy.

Thunbergia alata
BLACK-EYED SUSAN
Acanthaceae
H 5 – 10ft (1.5 – 3m)

Generally grown as a trailing annual, this plant is actually a climbing perennial. It produces a profusion of orange, yellow, or cream flowers with purple-brown centers throughout summer and fall. Since it is not hardy, protection is needed over winter, so growing it in a container will allow it to be moved indoors or into a conservatory or sunroom until the following year.

Lathyrus odoratus 'Spencer Hybrids mixed'

Clematis macropetala 'Maidwell Hall'

Jasminum humile 'Revolution'

Lonicera periclymenum 'Serotina'

Solanum crispum 'Glasnevin'

FEATURE PLANTS

Hydrangea macrophylla

Plants that have particularly handsome attributes of form can be described as having architectural merit. Even in small gardens, these striking plants have their uses. Just because a garden is limited in size does not mean that you have to think small in terms of plants. A good architectural plant, sited in a corner, alcove, or at a focal point in the garden, changes the dimensions of the garden and gives it a change of scale and pace.

By virtue of their size and form, these plants can be sited in solitary positions, often slightly raised above the rest of the plantings, to make a strong statement.

Among the best architectural foliage plants are those with either large leaves or interesting leaf forms. The sword- and fan-shaped leaves of yuccas, phormiums, and cordylines, which are often distinctively marked, look particularly good in raised containers. Equally strong in form are big artichokes and thistles, some well over 6ft 6in (2m) tall and with steely-blue foliage. Slightly softer in form are the tall shapes and softer leaves of the plume poppy (*Macleaya cordata*).

Of the architectural flowering plants, the big trumpet-shaped flowers of the tender Angel's trumpet (*Brugmansia* sp.) and the wonderfully scented, similarly trumpet-shaped flowers of *Lilium regale* make wonderful additions, in matched pairs, to a summer doorway or terraced patio.

On a smaller scale, the clump-forming, starry blue flowers of *Agapanthus* make excellent specimen container plants, as do the huge cloudlike heads of purple flowers and straplike leaves of the big allium, *A. christophii*.

Agapanthus
AFRICAN BLUE LILY
Alliaceae
H 16 – 48in (40 – 120cm)
S 12 – 24in (30 – 60cm)

These attractive, dramatic perennials form clumps of arching, straplike leaves of a rich green. The rounded flowerheads are produced on tall stems, with the individual bell- or trumpet-shaped flowers being held aloft or drooping down, according to variety. A. 'Liliput' and A. 'Midnight Blue,' with deep blue flowers, are smaller varieties suitable for growing in containers. A. 'Headbourne Hybrids' has funnel-shaped flowers in shades of purple, blue, and white.

Allium christophii
ONION
Alliaceae
H 12 – 24in (30 – 60cm)
S 6 – 7in (15 – 18cm)

The straplike, gray-green leaves of this perennial grow up from the bulbous base and are fringed with short, stiff hairs. These begin to die back almost before the globe-shaped flowerheads appear in early summer. Each head consists of up to 50 star-shaped, metallic, pinkish-purple flowers, which can be cut and dried for use in indoor flower arrangements. At 4 – 10in

(10 – 25cm) high, A. *karataviense* is smaller and one of the few onions whose leaves are as attractive as its flowers. Its size makes it ideal for smaller containers. Pairs of broad leaves grow from the basal bulb, each leaf forming a wide arc. The leaves are greenish-purple in color, with red edges. Umbels of pale pink, star-shaped flowers are borne in summer on red-tinted stems.

Brugmansia × candida
ANGEL'S TRUMPETS
Solanaceae
H 4 – 6ft (1.2 – 1.8m)
S 6 – 8ft (1.8 – 2.4m)

Brugmansia is not fully hardy outdoors, but will thrive in a protected position away from frost. It is a large plant, ideal for a conservatory, where its spectacular, fragrant, trumpet-shaped flowers can be fully appreciated. These are produced throughout summer and fall and come in shades of apricot (B. × c. 'Grand Marnier') and white (B. × c. 'Double White').

Canna × generalis
INDIAN SHOT PLANT
Cannaceae
H 5 – 7ft (1.5 – 2.2m)
S 20in (50cm)

Tall, exotic-looking herbaceous perennials with orchid-like flowers, growing from slowly-spreading rhizomes. They prefer moist soil in full sun, and

Agapanthus hybrid

Canna 'General Eisenhower'

provide color and height where space is limited. Numerous hybrids have foliage colors varying from green to bronze, and flower colors including yellow, orange, red, coral, and salmon. They will need protection over winter.

Cordyline australis
CABBAGE PALM
Agavaceae
H 3ft (1m) in pots **s** 3ft (1m)
A slow-growing, half-hardy tree, it can grow to 25ft (7m) when planted in soil. The strap-shaped leaves are borne at the tip of a narrow stem, and form an arching cluster. Older trees bear long plumelike panicles of creamy flowers in summer.

Fritillaria imperialis
CROWN IMPERIAL
Liliaceae
H 2 – 3ft (60 – 90cm)
s 18in (45cm)
This handsome spring-flowering bulb has lance-shaped green leaves, which curl over at the tip from the center of which a spire of tulip-shaped drooping flowers in yellow to orange-red is borne in mid-spring. Will do well in sun or partial shade.

Helianthus annuus
SUNFLOWER
Compositae
H 2 – 15ft (0.6 – 5m)
s up to 4ft (1.2m)
Sunflowers come in shades of gold, yellow, and orange, and in a wide range of heights. *H.a.* 'Sunspot' has 10in (25cm) yellow flowers on 2ft (60cm) stems; *H.a.* 'Teddy Bear' has 5in (13cm) double, deep-yellow flowers on 3ft (90cm) stems. Many are unbranching, although some, such as *H.a.* 'Music Box,' branch freely, and have numerous flowers.

Hydrangea macrophylla
COMMON HYDRANGEA
Hydrangeaceae
H 3 – 6ft (1 – 2m) **s** 5ft (1.5m)
Rounded, deciduous shrubs preferring moist soil. They are

divided into two groups according to the flowers: lace-caps (flattened clusters of tiny fertile flowers surrounded by a ring of larger sterile ones), such as 'Blue Wave,' and mopheads (or Hortensias, with a spherical head of larger sterile flowers), such as dark blue 'Europa.' Flower colors of blue, white, and pink are influenced by soil acidity, blue requiring the more acid soil.

Lilium regale
REGAL LILY
Liliaceae
H 2 – 6ft (0.6 – 1.8m)
s 6 – 8in (15 – 20cm)
From a dull-looking bulb, lilies produce the most spectacular flowers in summer. Those of the regal lily are large and trumpet-shaped, highly fragrant, and produced in clusters of up to 25 at the top of the stem. Pinkish in bud, they open white with a pinkish-purple reverse and yellow center with golden anthers. They prefer full sun and a well-drained soil.

Macleaya microcarpa
PLUME POPPY
Papaveraceae
H 7ft (2.2m) **s** 3ft (1m)
This rhizomatous perennial has graceful, heart-shaped, gray-green foliage and delicate grass-like flowers on tall stems. The tubelike, petal-less flowers are carried in plumes. *M.m.* 'Kelway's Coral Plume' has

coral-pink flowers in early summer. An invasive plant, it is best kept in a container, and will need regular repotting.

Melianthus major
HONEY BUSH
Melianthaceae
H 6 – 10ft (1.8 – 3m)
s 3 – 10ft (1 – 3m)
A strong specimen shrub with hollow stems set near ground level. It has spreading, gray- to blue-green pinnate leaves, each deeply toothed. The small, tube-shaped, deep brownish-red flowers are borne in early summer on tall spikes. Melianthus is not frost-hardy.

Phormium tenax
NEW ZEALAND FLAX
Phormiaceae
H 10ft (3m) **s** 4ft (1.2m)
A half-hardy evergreen perennial, *P. tenax* is grown for

its tall sword-shape leaves. *P.t.* 'Purpureum' has bronze-purple foliage and *P.t.* 'Variegatum' has yellow/green striped leaves. The flowers, a dull red, are carried in long panicles between summer and fall.

Yucca filamentosa
ADAM'S NEEDLE
Agavaceae
H 6ft (1.8m) **s** 5ft (1.5m)
A dramatic, stemless, evergreen shrub, forming a rosette of long, rigid, lance-shaped leaves of a dark green edged with curly white threads. A tall spike of white, bell-shaped flowers may be produced in summer. Grow in full sun. *Y.f.* 'Bright Edge' has yellow-edges to the leaves; *Y.f.* 'Variegata' has white-edged, blue-green leaves. *Y. gloriosa* has darker leaves and is larger. It flowers later in the year and only when about five years old.

Lilium regale

Melianthus major

Helianthus annuus

Macleaya microcarpa

Yucca gloriosa

FOLIAGE PLANTS

Often forgotten in the hectic rush to include flower color, foliage plays an essential part in giving a garden, no matter how small, a backcloth against which the flowers can be seen to full advantage, and where the leaves are particularly striking (see Feature Plants, pages 122-3), makes a valuable contribution to the overall design features of the garden.

Foliage comes in many forms, textures and colors. The selection here simply aims to give a taste of the myriad different types available, from the tiny evergreen leaves of boxwood (*Buxus sempervirens*) or the neat oval leaves of bay (*Laurus nobilis*), which lend themselves to being clipped into neat topiary forms, to the conical form of the dwarf cypress and the marvelous crenellate fronds of ferns such as *Asplenium* and *Polypodium*.

Many foliage plants will thrive in shady areas of the garden where you would have considerable difficulty persuading flowering plants to flourish. Among these are plants like ivy (*Hedera* sp.), which has a wonderfully diverse range of leaf forms from the long, narrow leaves of *Hedera sagittifolia* to the big, cream-splashed leaves of the more tender *Hedera helix* 'Glacier.'

Silvery felted leaves make a contribution to the dry garden, their furry coating enabling them to stand up well to drought. Many of these silver- or furry-leaved plants are herbs (wormwood and sage, for example) but the silvery-leaved senecios are excellent for containers and make a wonderful foil for purple- or blue-flowered plants.

Hedera helix 'Pedata'

Alchemilla mollis
LADY'S MANTLE
Rosaceae
H 24in (60cm)
S 30in (75cm)

A clump-forming perennial with rounded, soft green leaves which are covered with fine, silky hairs. It is drought-tolerant and makes an excellent ground-cover plant. Loose clusters of tiny, greenish-yellow flowers are produced throughout the summer. Grow the plant in moist soil in full sun or partial shade, and remove the dead flowerheads regularly to prevent seeding.

Asplenium scolopendrium
HART'S TONGUE FERN
Aspleniaceae
H 17 – 28in (45 – 70cm)
S 24in (60cm)

A distinctive evergreen fern, this plant has bright green, wavy, straplike fronds, with slightly frilled edges, a pointed tip, and a heart-shaped base. It is hardy, and enjoys a moist soil in partial shade. In a container, extra sand may be added to the soil mix to ensure adequate drainage. *A.s. Crispum* Group has very frilled edges to the leaves.

Buxus sempervirens
BOXWOOD, BOX
Buxaceae
H 10ft (3m)
S 4 – 6ft (1.2 – 1.8m)

A hardy, slow-growing, bushy evergreen plant with small, oval-shaped, glossy, dark green leaves. Often used for hedging, it is useful as a foil to more brightly colored plants, and attractive in its variegated forms of *B.s.* 'Elegantissima' (white-edged leaves) and *B.s.* 'Marginata' (yellow-edged leaves). Used singly in a container, its main attraction is that it can easily be clipped to form topiary.

Chamaecyparis
DWARF CYPRESS
Cupressaceae
H 3 – 5ft (1 – 1.5m)
S up to 3ft (1m)

Cypresses are ideal at providing structure in a plant display because they remain evergreen throughout the year. They come in all shapes, sizes, and colors, but where space is limited, only truly dwarf ones should be chosen. *C. lawsoniana* 'Minima' has blue-green foliage and a round habit. *C. obtusa* 'Nana Aurea' has golden foliage and a flattened, upright habit. *C. obtusa* 'Pygmaea' has green foliage in flattened sprays.

Euphorbia characias subsp. wulfenii
SPURGE
Euphorbiaceae
H and S 4ft (1.2m)

An upright, evergreen shrub with gray-green leaves on purple-tinted stems, preferring moist soil and partial shade. Each stem grows one year and flowers the next – and should then be cut off unless the seed is wanted. The unusual flowers are borne in rounded clusters at the tips of the stems, and are yellow-green in color. *E.c. subsp. characias* has handsome green flowers with deep purple centers.

Hedera helix
COMMON IVY
Araliaceae
H 4in (10cm)
S 3ft (1m) or more

The small-leaved ivies look exceptionally good in tall containers or hanging baskets, where they can trail gracefully. Choose varieties with leaves to complement the planting. All are tolerant of a wide range of conditions. *H.h.* 'Goldchild' has a broad yellow margin around each gray-green leaf, *H.h.* 'Eva' has small, gray-green leaves with creamy-white edges, and *H.h.* 'Ivalace' has wavy, glossy, dark

Asplenium scolopendrium

Buxus sempervirens

Euphorbia characias subsp. *wulfenii*

green leaves. (See also page 120, CLIMBERS AND WALL SHRUBS).

Heuchera micrantha 'Palace Purple'
CORAL FLOWER
Saxifragaceae
H 12 – 18in (30 – 45cm)
S 12in (30cm)

A herbaceous perennial, this is well worth growing for its handsome maplelike deep purple leaves and deep maroon flowers. Will cope with sun or partial shade but prefers light, well-drained soil. Use as either a container-grown feature plant or as edging.

Hosta sieboldiana 'Elegans'
PLANTAIN LILY
Funkiaceae
H 3ft (1m) S 4ft (1.2m)

A long-lived perennial which forms a clump of thick, ribbed, heart-shaped, blue-green leaves. Grows best in moist soil and partial shade (especially from noon sun). Bell-shaped, mauve flowers are produced on tall stems in summer. The slightly smaller variety, *H. s.* 'Frances Williams,' has gray-white flowers and thick, heart-shaped leaves, drawn around to form a cup. They are ribbed and puckered, blue-green in the center with a lighter yellow-green edge. Hostas associate

well with water, but will grow in containers as long as they are well watered and fertilized.

Laurus nobilis
BAY
Lauraceae
H 16ft (5m) S 10ft (3m)

As well as lending its distinctive, warm aroma to cooking, bay makes an attractive specimen plant and can be shaped as it grows into a pyramid, ball, or standard. It needs a sunny or partially-shaded position away from cold winds and, in colder areas, will need some winter protection. The leaves are aromatic, glossy, and dark green; the flowers are small and greenish-yellow.

Polypodium vulgare
COMMON POLYPODY
Polypodiaceae
H 12in (30cm) S indefinite

A typical evergreen fern, with arching, dark green fronds 16in (40cm) long, divided into oblong pinnae. It enjoys full sun or light shade among other plants, or standing alone as a specimen. Unlike some ferns, it is fully hardy, although protection may be needed around the base of the container in very low temperatures to protect the roots. The variety 'Cornubiense' is very vigorous, and makes good ground cover.

Senecio cineraria 'Silver Dust'
Compositae
H and S 12in (30cm)

An evergreen subshrub, usually grown as an annual and discarded at the end of the summer. The lacy, deeply-divided leaves are covered in a gray-white felt, giving the whole plant a silvery-white appearance. Small yellow flowers appear in the second summer after planting. *S.c.* 'Alice' has deeply cut silvery-white leaves; *S.c.* 'White Diamond' has oaklike grayish-white leaves. The plant prefers a sunny position and tolerates slightly dry conditions, so is good for hanging baskets.

Vinca minor
LESSER PERIWINKLE
Apocynaceae
H 4 – 8in (10 – 20cm)
S indefinite

A hardy, spreading evergreen, with long, trailing stems which root as they grow, bearing small, oval-shaped, dark green leaves and trumpet-shaped flowers of blue, purple, reddish-purple, or white. *V.m.* 'Azurea Flore Pleno' has double, light blue flowers. *V.m.* 'Gertrude Jekyll' is compact with white flowers. *V.m.* 'La Grave' has large, lavender-colored flowers.

Heuchera micrantha 'Palace Purple'

Hosta fortunei 'Francee'

TRAILING PLANTS

Among the most useful plants in a small garden are those with a trailing habit, both for foliage or flowers. They make excellent candidates for all forms of container, but particularly for hanging baskets where they can be persuaded to create wonderfully relaxed plantings, in a range of beautiful single colors and color mixtures.

Of the trailing flowering plants, some forms of begonia, geranium, petunia, convolvulus, lobelia, diascia, and felicia are highly popular flowering plants in a marvellous mixture of colors and flower shapes, from the tiny starry flowers of lobelia to the soft-petaled blooms of convolvulus, the waxy almost oriental quality of begonias, through to the rather blowzy big flowers of slightly scented petunias.

Of the trailing leaves, those of helichrysum, ivy, and vinca, as well as those of nasturtiums (*Tropaeolum majus*), can be used to soften the edges of containers, or trail elegantly from the top of walls, for example. Any mixed planting is most successful if the balance between foliage form and flower power is maintained.

Trailing petunias

Begonia
Begoniaceae

H 6 – 24in (15 – 60cm)

s 6 – 18in (15 – 45cm)

The trailing Pendulas (single to double) are excellent for containers or hanging baskets. Other summer-flowering begonias hardy enough to survive outdoors are the Tuberous Begonias, grouped as large-flowered Tuberhybridas (usually double-flowered), the smaller-flowered *Multifloras* (single to double), and *Semperflorens*, which are smaller, with a profusion of (usually) single flowers. Foliage is green to bronze, and flower shades include red, pink, orange, yellow, and white, depending on variety.

Brachyscome
SWAN RIVER DAISY
Compositae

H 12 – 18in (30 – 45cm)

s 14 – 18in (35 – 45cm)

Delicately leaved plants, which produce masses of small, daisy-like flowers in summer. They are fairly drought-tolerant, making them useful in hanging baskets. *B. iberidifolia* is bushy or spreading, with soft, gray foliage and fragrant blue, pink, or white, yellow-centered flowers. *B.i.* Splendor Series has white, pink, or purple, black-centered flowers. *B. multifida* produces fewer flowers in blue, pink, mauve, purple, and white.

Convolvulus sabatius
BINDWEED
Convolvulaceae

H 6in (15cm) **s** 20in (50cm)

A tolerant, slender, trailing perennial, sometimes grown as an annual, with small, bright green leaves and funnel-shaped flowers, ranging from very pale to rich, deep purple-blue. These are produced in clusters of up to three throughout the summer and early fall. Overwinter in a cold greenhouse for cuttings or division in spring. Smaller,

Begonia semperflorens

bushy varieties of convolvulus thrive in containers. *C. cneorum* has silky, silver-colored leaves and flowers which are pink in bud, opening white. It prefers a sunny, well-drained site and needs frost protection. (See also page 120, CLIMBERS AND WALL SHRUBS).

Diascia
Scrophulariaceae

H up to 12in (30cm)

s 8 – 12in (20 – 30cm)

Trailing or upright, pretty evergreen, or semi-evergreen, mat-forming perennials. They prefer a sunny site and have a long flowering season, bearing a profusion of tubular flowers with backward-facing spurs. *D.* 'Pink Queen' trails, bearing masses of pink, long-spurred flowers; *D. rigescens* is more upright, with deep pink flowers; and *D.* 'Ruby Field' is more compact, with rich, salmon-pink flowers.

Felicia
BLUE DAISY
Compositae

H 12 – 24in (30 – 60cm)

Grown mainly for their outstanding display of long-stalked, daisylike flowers with yellow centers, these are excellent plants for the hanging basket because they enjoy slightly dry conditions and a sunny position. *F. amelloides* is a small, bushy subshrub with deep

Brachyscome multifida

Convolvulus sabatius

Felicia amelloides

green leaves and light to dark blue flowers throughout summer and early fall. *F.a.* 'Read's White' has white flowers, *F.a.* 'Santa Anita' produces large, vivid blue flowers, and *F. amoena* 'Variegata' has cream-marked leaves and blue flowers.

Fuchsia
Onagraceae

H 6 – 12in (15 – 30cm)
S 18 – 24in (46 – 60cm)

Choose only very small trailing types (or bush fuchsias) for use in hanging baskets. Tolerant of full sun or partial shade, they prefer shelter from cold winds. *F.* 'Marinka' is a trailing variety with dark green leaves and shaded red flowers. *F.* 'Lady Thumb' is a small upright bush with small, semidouble flowers of rose-pink and white.

Helichrysum petiolare
Compositae

H up to 6in (15cm)
S 24in (60cm)

A frost-tender, trailing, evergreen shrub with branching stems and wooly, heart-shaped leaves. Grown mainly for its pretty foliage, it does produce small whitish flowers in late summer. Prefers a sheltered position in full sun, and will tolerate slightly dry conditions. *H.p.* 'Aurea' (syn. *H.p.* 'Limelight') has bright, lime-green foliage, *H.p.* 'Variegatum'

has gray-green leaves, variegated with cream. *H. p.* 'Silverlight' has felted gray leaves.

Impatiens
See page 132, SEASONAL COLOR

Lantana camara
Verbenaceae

H and **S** 3ft (1m)

The leaves of this sun-loving, evergreen shrub are rough and dull green, but the clusters of flowers are bright and colorful, changing from pale yellow to salmon, red, and purple as they age. *L.c.* 'Cream Carpet' is smaller, with creamy white flowers, *L.c.* 'Feston Rose' has pink and yellow flowerheads, and *L.c.* 'Goldmine' has golden yellow flowerheads.

Lobelia erinus
Campanulaceae

H 4 – 9in (10 – 23cm)
S 4 – 6in (10 – 15cm)

Bushy, low-growing, or trailing plants grown as annuals with green or bronze foliage, bearing masses of small white, pink, red, violet, purple, or blue flowers throughout summer and fall. *L.e. Cascade* and Regatta Series are both trailing, *L.e.* 'Crystal Palace' has dark blue flowers, *L.e.* 'Rosamund' has cherry-red flowers with a white center and *L.e.* 'Minstrel' has bright blue flowers with a white center.

Helichrysum petiolare 'Silverlight'

Lantana camara 'Goldmine'

Lobelia 'Minstrel'

127

Variegated pelargonium

Petunia 'Vogue'

Tropaeolum 'Apricot Twist'

Verbena 'Silver Anne'

Mimulus
MONKEY FLOWER
Scrophulariaceae
H 6 – 12in (15 – 30cm)
S 12in (30cm)
Bushy, spreading plants, perennial or annual, which enjoy a warm, sunny position. They produce trumpet-shaped flowers throughout the summer. Tender *M.* × *hybridus* cultivars, including 'Calypso,' bear single-colored, spotted, and bicolored flowers in red, pink, orange, and yellow, and the Magic Series includes unusual pastel shades as well as bright oranges, yellows, and reds. M. 'Wisley Red' has velvety, dark red flowers.

Pelargonium
GERANIUM
Geraniaceae
H and S up to 18in (45cm)
The trailing ivy-leaved geraniums are especially useful in pots or hanging baskets. Their foliage may be plain, variegated with cream or yellow

or marked with red. Flower colors include red, salmon, pink, violet, or white. They are tolerant of a range of conditions, although they prefer full sun or partial shade. P. 'L'Elégante' has cream-variegated silvery green leaves, which turn purplish if the plant is dry. P. 'Abel Carriere' has semidouble light purple flowers. P. 'Jacky' has semidouble lavender pink flowers and small leaves. (See also page 133, SEASONAL COLOR: SUMMER).

Petunia
Solanaceae
H up to 12in (30cm)
S up to 3ft (1m)
Tolerant, reliable plants, which produce flowers constantly throughout the summer, preferably in full sun and sheltered from cold winds. Cascade Series has long, trailing stems. *Grandiflora* petunias have fewer, larger flowers than *Multiflora* types, which are more

bushy, with plenty of smaller flowers. P. 'Celebrity Chiffon Morn' has soft, salmon-pink flowers, P. 'Prism Sunshine' has large, light yellow flowers, and P. 'Vogue' has large light mauve flowers.

Scaevola aemula
FAIRY FAN FLOWER
Goodeniaceae
H 6in (15cm) S 5ft (1.5m)
An evergreen perennial, usually grown as an annual, with slightly hairy trailing or upright stems. The fan-shaped flowers are borne during the summer, and are blue to purple-blue. *S.a.* 'Blue Wonder' has vigorous trailing stems and a profusion of lilac-blue flowers all summer. S. 'Mauve Clusters' also has a trailing habit, and lilac-mauve flowers during summer and early fall.

Thunbergia alata
See page 121, CLIMBERS AND WALL SHRUBS

Tropaeolum majus
NASTURTIUM
Tropaeolaceae
H 3 – 10ft (1 – 3m)
S 5 – 10ft (1.5 – 3m)
A vigorous trailing or climbing plant with rounded, light green leaves and spurred flowers throughout summer and fall in shades of yellow, orange, and red. The flowers are edible and look wonderful in a salad. *T.* Alaska Series are dwarf, bushy annuals with cream-flecked leaves and yellow, orange, cream, and brown-red. *T.* 'Peach Melba' has semi-double yellow flowers with orange-red centers. *T.* 'Apricot Twist' is double-flowered.

Verbena
Verbenaceae
H 8in (20cm) S 3ft (1m)
Spreading perennials with toothed, mid-green leaves and masses of red, salmon, pink, white, purple, or yellow flowers in the summer, borne in flattened clusters. They prefer a sunny position and need winter protection. V. 'Lawrence Johnson' has rich red flowers in large clusters. V. 'Sissinghurst' has dark green leaves and magenta-pink flowers. V. 'Loveliness' has flowers of a pale lavender color. V. 'Silver Anne' produces bright pink, sweetly scented flowers, which fade to silver-white as they age.

Vinca minor
See page 125, FOLIAGE PLANTS

SPREADING PLANTS

Small spreading plants are ideal for filling in small corners, cracks, and crevices, but they can be used equally well in small containers as special interest plants in a miniature setting. Little pots of sedums with their succulent leaves make a wonderful textural contribution, while the small brilliantly colored flowers of aubrieta, in mauves, pinks, or blues, cascade from the top of any wall. The little silvery deadnettle (*Lamium maculatum* 'Beacon Silver') makes an excellent foil for mauve flowers, while *Tiarella cordifollia* will spread and do well in shade. Erigeron makes an excellent crevice-filler. It will grow in between the cracks in paving stones, softening their appearance, and will survive being crushed underfoot.

Erigeron glaucus

Ajuga reptans
BUGLE
Labiatae
H 4 – 12in (2 – 30cm)
S 12in (30cm)
This little creeping perennial makes excellent ground cover or edging. It has deep green oblong leaves and blue flowers in summer. A purple-leaved variety, 'Burgundy Glow,' is particularly attractive. It does best in partial shade.

Alyssum
Cruciferae
H 4 – 6in (10 – 15cm)
S 24in (60cm)
Mat- or clump-forming evergreen perennials, with gray-green leaves and tiny, yellow or white flowers in early summer. Prefers full sun and well-drained soil. *A. montanum* 'Berggold' has golden flowers, *A. spinosum* has white flowers and silvery leaves, and *A.s. var. roseum* has pale to deep rose-pink flowers.

Ajuga reptans

Arabis caucasica
ROCK CRESS
Cruciferae
H 6in (15cm) S 20in (50cm)
A vigorous, evergreen, mat-forming perennial, which is fully hardy and will grow well in any well-drained soil in full sun. Loose clusters of fragrant, white flowers are produced in late spring above the gray-green foliage. *A.c.* 'Flore Pleno' has double flowers, *A.c.* 'Variegata' has green leaves with yellow edges. *A. × arendsii* 'Rosabella' has deep rose-pink flowers.

Aubrieta × cultorum
AUBRETIA
Cruciferae
H 2in (5cm) S 24in (60cm)
Evergreen, spreading perennials with mid-green leaves and four-petaled flowers in spring. Grow in full sun in a well-drained soil on banks or walls. Forms include 'Argenteovariegata' (white leaf edging, single mauve flowers), 'Aureovariegata' (gold-edged leaves, single mauve flowers), 'Bressingham Pink' (double pink flowers), 'Joy' (double mauve flowers), and 'J.S. Baker' (single purple flowers with white eyes).

Erigeron
FLEABANE
Compositae
H 2 – 24in (5 – 60cm)
S 12 – 18in (30 – 45cm)
Ranging from small alpines to taller clump-forming species, they prefer full sun and a moist soil. *E. karvinskianus* is a vigorous, carpeting perennial with yellow-centered flowers that open white and fade to pink. *E. chrysopsidis* 'Grand Ridge' is mat-forming and dense, with deep-yellow flowers produced during the summer. *E. glaucus* has pale mauve flowers with yellow centers from late spring to summer.

Lamium maculatum
DEAD NETTLE
Labiatae
H 8in (20cm) S 3ft (1m)
A low-growing, spreading perennial with medium-large, heart-shaped, toothed leaves, often marked with splashes of other colors. The flowers appear in late spring, but the foliage is attractive in a hanging basket. Tolerates partial shade. *L.m. album* has silvery markings on the leaves, *L.m.* 'Aureum' has yellow leaves with whitish centers, and *L.m.* 'Beacon Silver' has silver leaves with a narrow green edge.

Sedum
STONECROP
Crassulaceae
H 10in (25cm) S 18in (45cm)
Hardy, mat-forming perennials bearing star-shaped yellow or white flowers in summer and fall. They prefer full sun and neutral to alkaline soil. *S. acre* is very low-growing, with yellow flowers. *S.* 'Ruby Glow' has red stems and green-purple leaves and red flowers during summer and fall. *S. spectabile* (ice plant) is taller, producing flattened heads of pink flowers above succulent-looking leaves.

Sempervivum
HOUSELEEK
Crassulaceae
H 3 – 4in (8 – 10cm)
S 12in (30cm)
Hardy, mat-forming perennials with rosettes of succulent leaves, sometimes covered with fine white webbing. Flat heads of star-shaped flowers, of yellow, white, red, or purple are produced in summer. Grow in full sun in a well-drained soil. *S. arachnoideum* has reddish-colored leaves and pink flowers. *S. giuseppii* has bright green leaves with red tips and red flowers.

Tiarella cordifolia
FOAM FLOWER
Saxifragaceae
H 4 – 12in (10 – 30cm)
S 12 – 18in (30 – 45cm)
A vigorous, hardy, herbaceous perennial which is excellent as ground cover and also in hanging baskets. It spreads by means of stolons, and prefers cool, moist (but not water-logged) conditions and partial or full shade. The low-growing, lobed, heart-shaped leaves are pale green, turning reddish in fall. Loose spikes of tiny, creamy white flowers are produced throughout summer.

SEASONAL COLOR

Winter-flowering cyclamen

The main aim in any small space is to make sure that there is something of interest, in terms of flowers or foliage, at different times of the year. A garden that has only one flowering season is very dismal for the rest of the year, and in a small space it is particularly important to ensure that you have a good spread of continuous flower color, although inevitably winter has less to offer than summer.

Spring, nonetheless, with its selection of spring bulbs, in clear colors and with fresh green leaves, offers a wide range of choice from the first snowdrops and crocuses through to the tiny, sweetly scented little narcissus, small brilliantly colored tulips and little starry scillas in the form of bulbs, with primulas and violas playing an equally important role in mid-spring.

Summer offers a marvelous range of flowering plants, some annuals, some perennials, and some flowering shrubs. Little scented pinks, exotic-looking gazanias, and brilliant colored daisies and marigolds all help to create a highly colorful summer pageant, backed up with the gentler shades of more cloudlike flowers of shrubs like catmint. Small patio roses have been increasingly bred, providing a wide choice of sufficiently small roses for tiny balconies or even windowsills.

Fall and winter have a smaller range of plants to offer, but their very scarcity makes them a great joy to behold. The dying embers of summer are echoed in the bright colors of chrysanthemums and dahlias in fall. Little cyclamen, with their delicately marked deep green leaves, the tiny winter iris, *I. unguicularis*, and little winter-flowering pansies and scented shrubs like mahonia and witch hazel help to perfume the garden in winter.

SPRING

Convallaria majalis
LILY OF THE VALLEY
Convallariaceae
H 9in (23cm) **S** 2in (5cm)

Hardy perennials with large, oval, pointed leaves, preferring partial shade, and spreading by means of rhizomatous, underground stems. Produces upright stalks bearing hanging, waxy, bell-like flowers in spring. They are wonderfully fragrant. *C.m.* 'Albostriata' has cream-striped leaves, *C.m.* 'Flore Pleno' has double flowers, and *C.m. var. rosea* produces flowers which are a pale mauve-pink.

Crocus
Iridaceae
H up to 4in (10cm)
S 1 – 2in (2.5 – 5cm)

Small, spring- or fall-flowering plants, which grow from individual corms. Long, slender leaves are sometimes white-striped along the upper surface. Flowers are goblet-shaped, produced four or more per corm, in shades of white, yellow, blue, and purple, sometimes in combination on the same plant. *C. chrysanthus, C. corsicus, C. gargaricus, C. minimus,* and their hybrids all flower in spring. *C. × luteus* 'Dutch Yellow' is a vigorous spring-flowering crocus which needs full sun.

Erysimum (syn. Cheiranthus)
WALLFLOWER
Cruciferae
H 10 – 32in (25 – 80cm)
S 12 – 16in (30 – 40cm)

Colorful, reliable, and hardy, wallflowers produce a brilliant display in spring. Flower colors include yellow, orange, red, and mauve. Cultivars of *E. cheiri,* such as Bedder Series, are more compact. *E.* 'Bowles Mauve' is a perennial with mauve flowers. *E. × kewense* 'Harpur Crewe' has double yellow flowers.

Galanthus nivalis
SNOWDROP
Amaryllidaceae
H up to 9in (23cm)
S 1.5 – 3in (4 – 8cm)

Bulbous perennials, producing long, straplike leaves and drooping flowers in spring before dying down and becoming dormant. They need a constantly moist soil, preferably in partial shade. Varieties are single, double, such as *G.n.* 'Flore Pleno,' or unusually marked, such as *G.n.* 'Lady Elphinstone,' which has yellow markings on the inner sepals on established plants.

Helleborus
HELLEBORE
Ranunculaceae
H and **S** to 2ft (60cm) or more

Rhizomatous perennials, either producing deciduous leaves from the base, or biennial stems. Soil preference varies, but all prefer partial shade. *H. argutifolius* has sharply toothed leaves and pale green flowers, *H. foetidus* has dark green leaves and purple-edged pale green flowers, *H. niger* (Christmas rose) has large, open, white flowers, sometimes tinted pink or green. *H. orientalis* (Lenten rose) has greenish-white or purple flowers.

Convallaria majalis

Iris
Iridaceae

H up to 12in (30cm)

S 4in (10cm)

Bulbous iris tend to flower before early rhizomatous ones; both types need a well-drained soil and full sun. Producing one flower per bulb, *I. reticulata* has pale to deep violet-blue or red-purple petals with a yellow marking on each fall (lower petal), and *I. danfordiae* has yellow with green markings. Hybrids include *I.* 'Apollo' (cream and yellow) and *I.* 'Harmony' (royal blue).

Muscari
GRAPE HYACINTH

Hyacinthaceae

H 8in (20cm) S 2in (5cm)

Bulbous perennials, which produce long, narrow, fleshy leaves and spikes of bell-shaped flowers in spring. They enjoy full sun, and clumps should be divided regularly. *M. armeniacum* bears bright blue flowers, those of its form *M.a.* 'Blue Spike' are double. *M. aucheri* 'Tubergenianum' has blue flowers with a crown of sterile florets, while those of *M. botryoides* 'Album' are white and fragrant.

Narcissus
DAFFODIL

Amaryllidaceae

H 6 – 24in (15 – 60cm)

Bulbous perennials, producing long, straplike leaves and stems bearing between one and 20 flowers, usually yellow or white, occasionally with red, orange, or pink. Of the hundreds of hybrids, *N.* 'Rip van Winkle' is small, producing double, yellow flowers with pointed petals; *N.* 'St Keverne' is tall, with single, rich golden flowers; and *N.* 'Scarlet Gem' bears clusters of fragrant yellow flowers with orange centers. *N.* 'Peeping Tom' produces dainty flowers.

Primula
Primulaceae

H 8in (20cm)

S 10 – 14in (25 – 35cm)

Many species and hybrid primulas flower in spring, giving a colorful display of red, orange, yellow, white, pink, or purple. They are tolerant of sun or partial shade, but need a moist soil. *P. vulgaris* (primrose) is a rosette-forming perennial, with single flowers on short stems. In the wild these are pale yellow, but cultivated forms are available in many colors: *P.v.* 'Jack in the Green' has yellow flowers backed by green bracts; *P.v.* subsp. *sibthorpii* has rose-pink, red, white, or purple flowers; *P. auricula* produces clusters of fragrant, deep yellow flowers on a tall stem. Other forms have red or purple flowers

Erysimum 'Bowles Mauve'

Crocus × *luteus* 'Dutch Yellow'

Muscari armeniacum

with a yellow center, such as *P.a.* 'Mark' (wine-red and yellow), and *P.a.* 'Adrian' (purple-blue and pale yellow).

Rhododendron (and Azalea)
Ericaceae

H 3 – 12ft (1 – 4m)

Preferring acid soil, rhododendrons and azaleas flower throughout spring, from early *R.* 'Praecox' (rose-purple), to dwarf mid-season azaleas such as *R.* 'Hino-mayo' (pink flowers), and the superb *R. yakushimanum* (rich pink in bud, opening paler and fading to white, with cinnamon-colored down on the leaves). Flower colors include shades of white, pink, orange, red, purple, and yellow, and preference for sun or partial shade varies between species.

Scilla siberica
SIBERIAN SQUILL

Hyacinthaceae

H 4 – 8in (10 – 20cm)

S 2in (5cm)

A delicate-looking (but quite hardy), bulbous perennial with long, slender leaves and bright blue, wide bell- or bowl-shaped

Narcissus 'Peeping Tom'

Scilla siberica

flowers carried in clusters of 4-5 on dark green stems. *S.s.* 'Alba' has white flowers; *S.s.* 'Spring Beauty' has deep blue flowers. Grow in full sun or partial shade, and allow to dry during summer dormancy.

Tulipa
TULIP

Liliaceae

H 8 – 24in (20 – 60cm)

S 6 – 8in (15 – 20cm)

Bulbous perennials which vary widely in leaf and flower color, shape, and size. Flowers are generally cup-shaped with six overlapping petals, and may be borne singly or in clusters of up to 12. *T. fosteriana* and hybrids have single bowl-shaped flowers, white, yellow, or red, sometimes with a contrasting-colored base and margins. The leaves are often marked with red-purple. *T. purissima*, formerly *T.* 'White Emperor,' in the Fosteriana group, has pure white flowers. In the Greigii group, *T.* 'Red Riding Hood' has bright scarlet flowers and maroon-marked leaves. *T. kaufmanniana* (water-lily tulip) has wide-spreading cream-yellow flowers flushed pink, orange, or red outside. *T. praestans* bears clusters of up to five orange-red flowers. *T. clusiana* has white flowers, striped pink on the outside. Prefers full sun and shelter.

Viola
VIOLET

Violaceae

H 4in (10cm)

Low-growing perennials with heart-shaped leaves and dainty flowers, which will grow in full sun or partial shade. *V. canina* (wild violet) has blue, violet, or white flowers. *V. cornuta* has violet-blue flowers with white markings. *V. labradorica* has bronze-purple young foliage and purple flowers. *V. tricolor* self-seeds freely and produces flowers from spring to fall which combine purple, lavender, white, and yellow tints.

V. bicolor is a dwarf, creeping perennial with yellow flowers.

131

SUMMER

Ageratum houstonianum
FLOSS FLOWER

Compositae

H and **s** 6 – 12in (15 – 30cm)

Butterflies love the long-lasting, fluffy-looking flowerheads of ageratum, in their shades of blue, pink, and white. Tolerant of slightly dry conditions, grow them in a sunny, sheltered position, perhaps as edging plants. *A.h.* 'Bavaria' has blue and white flowers, *A.h.* 'Hawaii White' has white flowers, *A.h.* 'Pacific' are a deep violet-blue, and those of *A.h.* 'Swing Pink' are bright candy-pink. *A.h.* 'Blue Danube' produces numerous lavender-blue flowers.

Armeria
THRIFT, SEA PINK

Plumbaginaceae

H 12 – 20in (30 – 50cm)

s 10 – 12in (25 – 30cm)

Hardy, tolerant plants which thrive in full sun in any soil, as long as it is well-drained. Good edging plants, they are cushion-forming, with slender, straplike leaves, and flowers carried in rounded heads during late spring to early summer. *A. juniperifolia* has purple-pink to white flowers. *A. maritima* has red-purple, pink, or white flowers; the form 'Bloodstone' has dark red flowers, and 'Vindictive' has rosy-pink flowers.

Bellis perennis
DAISY

Compositae

H and **s** 2 – 8in (5 – 20cm)

A rosette-forming perennial with bright green, rounded leaves, which will grow in most situations, and will seed itself readily unless regularly dead-headed. It produces red, pink, or white flowers with yellow centers throughout spring and summer. The Pomponette Series has double flowers up to 1.5in (4cm) across, and the Tasso Series has double flowers up to 2.5in (6cm) across.

Calendula officinalis
MARIGOLD

Compositae

H 12 – 24in (30 – 60cm)

s 12 – 18in (30 – 45cm)

Hardy annuals which self-seed readily, and thrive in full sun and poor soil. Single or double daisy-like flowers, up to 4in (10cm) across, are produced all summer, in shades of orange, yellow, and cream with a purple or brown center. *C.o.* 'Fiesta Gitana' is dwarf, with double, pale yellow or orange flowers. *C.o.* 'Indian Prince' has brown-tinted, dark orange flowers.

Dianthus
PINK

Caryophyllaceae

H 10 – 18in (25 – 45cm)

s 16in (40cm)

Evergreen, mound-forming perennials which prefer alkaline conditions in full sun. Flowers are single, semidouble, or double, with up to six blooms per stem, and of many color combinations. *D.* 'Gran's Favorite' has clove-scented white flowers with mauve edgings and centers. *D.* 'Doris' has fragrant, double flowers of pale pink with darker centers. *D.* 'Mrs Sinkins' has fragrant, double, fringed white flowers.

Dictamnus albus
BURNING BUSH

Rutaceae

H 16 – 36in (40 – 90cm)

s 24in (60cm)

A clump-forming perennial with divided, lemon-scented leaves. Tall, loose spikes of white or pink-tinted flowers with long stamens are produced in early summer. Grows well in any soil, and in full sun or partial shade. *D.a.* var. *purpureus* has mauve flowers with darker veins.

Gazania
Compositae

H 8 – 10in (20 – 25cm)

s 10in (25cm)

Annuals or half-hardy perennials with hairy, gray-green leaves. The large, daisylike flowers

Ageratum houstonianum 'Blue Danube'

come in shades of red, orange, yellow, and white. They enjoy well-drained soil and full sun, and are ideal for containers. G. Chansonette Series is perennial, bearing flowers with a darker central ring. G. Daybreak Series has glossy foliage; G. Mini-star Series is compact; and G. Talent Series is vigorous.

Geranium
CRANESBILL

Geraniaceae

H 6 – 24in (15 – 60cm)

s 12 – 36in (30 – 90cm)

Versatile, tolerant, hardy plants which will grow in almost any situation. The widely varying flowers are in shades of purple, blue, pink, or white. *G. cinereum* is a dwarf, rosette-forming perennial with white or pink purple-veined flowers. *G. himalayense* 'Gravetye' has blue flowers with a white center surrounded by purple-red. Low-growing *G. sanguineum* bears magenta flowers all summer; *G.s.* 'Album' is pure white. G. Johnson's Blue' has lavender-blue flowers with pink-tinged centers.

Gladiolus
Iridaceae

H 1.5 – 5.5ft (0.45 – 1.7m)

s 2 – 6in (5 – 15cm)

Upright, sun-loving, perennials that grow from a corm to produce a spike of funnel-shaped flowers, opening from the base up. Plant in groups for impact. *G. callianthus* produces fragrant, white flowers with purple-red centers in late summer. *G. cardinalis* bears red flowers

Armeria maritima

Bellis perennis

with white markings; G. 'Christabel' has yellow flowers with purple markings; and G. *byzantinus* produces magenta flowers in early summer.

Impatiens
BUSY LIZZIE

Balsaminaceae

H and **s** 12in (30cm)

Reliable and tolerant, the busy lizzie will flower throughout the summer, preferring shelter, partial shade, and moist conditions. *I. balsamina* is a slightly hairy, bushy plant bearing red, pink, purple, or white flowers – the Tom Thumb group are dwarf with large, double flowers. *I.* New Guinea Hybrids have gold-splashed, bronze or green foliage and bearing purple, red, salmon, pink, or white flowers.

Lychnis
CAMPION

Caryophyllaceae

H 6 – 48in (15 – 120cm)

s 6 – 18in (15 – 45cm)

Ranging from the dwarf to the tall, with flower colors including

Calendula officinalis

Dictamnus albus

Geranium 'Johnson's Blue'

Nicotiana × *sanderae*

red, pink, and white, Lychnis are varied and tolerant perennials. *L.* × *arkwrightii* 'Vesuvius' bears bright scarlet flowers amid bronze foliage. *L. chalcedonica* has rounded clusters of red flowers, while *L. coronaria* is widely branched, with wooly-gray leaves and magenta or white flowers. *L. flosjovis* is mat-forming, with pink, white, or scarlet flowers.

Nepeta
CATMINT
Labiatae
H 18 – 36in (45 – 90cm)
S 18 – 24in (45 – 60cm)

These clump-forming perennials enjoy well-drained soil in full sun or partial shade. Two-lipped flowers are borne in spikes, in shades of white, blue, and purple. *N.* × *faassenii* has silvery, aromatic leaves and pale lavender flowers. *N. sibirica* is upright and leafy, with blue flowers. *N.* 'Six Hills Giant' is hardy and vigorous, with blue flowers. *N.* 'Souvenir d'André Chaudron' is smaller, with darker flowers.

Nicotiana
TOBACCO PLANT
Solanaceae
H 9 – 24in (23 – 60cm)
S 10 – 14in (25 – 35cm)

Half-hardy annuals bearing trumpet-shaped flowers. Grow in full sun. *N.* × *sanderae* is an upright annual with open panicles of flowers in shades of red, pink, purple, or white. Domino Series has upward-facing flowers in combinations of red, pink, white, lime-green, and purple. Havana Series

Gazania 'Tiger'

plants are compact, and the Merlin Series is ideal for containers because it is dwarf.

Osteospermum
Compositae
H and **s** 18 – 24in (45 – 60cm)

Evergreen subshrubs or perennials, grown for their large, daisylike flowers of yellow, pink, purple, or white, often with darker centers. *O.* 'Buttermilk' is upright, with butter-yellow petals, flushed white at the center and edged bronze. *O. jucundum* has gray-green leaves and magenta flowers with purple centers which age to gold. *O.* 'Whirligig' has crimped white petals which are blue beneath, with a purple-blue center.

Pelargonium
GERANIUM
Geraniaceae
H 8 – 18in (20 – 45cm)
S 6 – 12in (15 – 30cm)

A huge group of plants which are generally half-hardy, flower profusely all summer, and are ideal as bedding or in containers, especially hanging baskets. Of

Impatiens hybrid

the upright geraniums – Regal, Zonal, Scented-leaved, and Unique – *P.* 'Lord Bute' (Regal) has clusters of dark reddish-black flowers; *P.* 'Sefton' (Regal) has cerise and deep red flowers; *P.* 'Ann Hoysted' (Zonal) has deep red flowers; *P.* 'Mabel Grey' (Scented-leaved) has strongly lemon-scented leaves and mauve flowers; while *P.* 'Voodoo (Unique) bears clusters of wine-red flowers with purple-black markings. (See also page 128, TRAILING PLANTS).

Rosa
MINIATURE & PATIO ROSES
Rosaceae
H 6 – 24in (15 – 60cm)
S 12in (30cm)

A group of small, bushy roses, which produce masses of small, double flowers throughout summer and fall. They are ideal in containers or small borders and as edging, in sunny positions. Patio roses are also available as short standards on stems up to 36in (90cm). *R.* 'Baby Masquerade' has double, yellow-pink flowers, *R.* 'Darling

Flame' has double, orange-red flowers, and *R.* 'Top Gear' has red flowers with white markings.

Rudbeckia
CONEFLOWER
Compositae
H 24 – 36in (60 – 90cm)
S 18 – 36in (45 – 90cm)

Annuals, biennials, and perennials, which enjoy moist soil in full sun or partial shade. Daisylike flowers in shades of yellow, orange, and red are produced through summer and fall. *R. fulgida* has yellow flowers with dark brown centers; var. *deamii* and var. *sullivantii* 'Goldsturm' are both shorter, the latter having large, golden-yellow flowers. *R. hirta* is biennial, with forms including 'Kelvedon Star,' 'Marmalade,' and 'Rustic Dwarfs.'

Salvia
SAGE
Labiatae
H 16 – 36in (40 – 90cm)
S 12 – 24in (30 – 60cm)

A widely varied group of frost- and fully hardy plants. Two-lipped flowers are borne on spikes, and foliage is often aromatic. *S. greggii* (autumn sage) is a dwarf evergreen shrub with pairs of purple, red, pink, yellow, or violet flowers. *S.g.* 'Raspberry Royal' has raspberry-colored flowers. *S. patens* is a tuberous perennial with deep blue flowers, while *S.p.* 'Cambridge Blue' is paler.

FALL & WINTER

Chrysanthemum
Compositae

H 24 – 30in (60 – 75cm)
S 12in (30cm)

Bushy annuals and herbaceous perennials, grown for their showy, fragrant flowers in late summer and fall. Grow in full sun in a well-drained soil. *C. carinatum* is an upright annual with daisylike flowers of yellow or white with purple centers. *C.c.* 'Court Jesters' bears flowers of white, yellow, orange, red ,and maroon, zoned with red or orange. *C.* 'Mary Stoker' has single, apricot-yellow flowers.

Cyclamen
SOWBREAD
Primulaceae

H 2 – 5in (5 – 12cm)
S 4 – 6in (10 – 15cm)

Tuberous perennials, which need a warm, dry summer dormancy, so are ideal for the rock garden, raised bed, or container. *C. cilicium* has white or pink flowers in fall. *C. coum* has rounded leaves, plain deep green or patterned with silver-green, and nodding flowers with reflexed petals in shades of pink and carmine-red in winter. *C. hederifolium* flowers in mid- to late fall, in shades of pink.

Daphne bholua
Thymelaeceae

H 6 – 12ft (2 – 4m) **S** 5ft (1.5m)

An upright shrub with leathery, oval-shaped, dark green leaves. Prefers cool, moist roots and slightly alkaline soil, and full sun or partial shade. The heavily fragrant, white-flushed pink flowers are produced in clusters at the ends of the shoots in winter, followed by round, purple-black fruits. *D.b.* 'Gurkha' is deciduous and very hardy. *D.b.* 'Jacqueline Postill' is evergreen with large flowers, white inside, purple-pink outside.

Gaultheria (Pernettya)
Ericaceae

H to 3ft (1m) **S** to 5ft (1.5m)

Hardy, evergreen shrubs with small, oval, pointed, glossy dark green leaves on slender red stems. Flowers in late spring are followed in fall by clusters of long-lasting bright, round fruits. *G. mucronata* has varieties with berries in red and pale lilac; others are white, pink, purple, or blue.

Hamamelis
WITCH HAZEL
Hamamelidaceae

H and **S** 12ft (4m)

Hardy shrubs, preferring neutral to acid soil and shelter, bearing small, fragrant, spidery flowers during winter, and having wonderful fall leaf colors. *H. × intermedia* bears yellow, orange, or red flowers; its form 'Diane' has dark-red flowers and 'Jelena' has copper-orange flowers (both have fiery fall foliage). *H. mollis* has golden-yellow flowers – its form 'Sandra' has purple young foliage, good fall tints, and dark yellow flowers.

Iris unguicularis
Iridaceae

H up to 12in (30cm)
S 4in (10cm)

A vigorous, rhizomatous iris, bearing large, fragrant pale- to deep-purple flowers with yellow markings on short stems. They appear in late winter and early spring. *I.u.* 'Alba' has white flowers with yellow markings. *I.u.* 'Mary Barnard' has bright violet flowers in midwinter. Grow in full sun in a well-drained, neutral to alkaline soil, preferably with some shelter.

Mahonia
Berberidaceae

H and **S** 3 – 12ft (1 – 4m)

Hardy shrubs, preferring full or partial shade, with prickly, leathery, pinnate leaves and spikes of bright yellow, sweetly scented flowers in winter. *M. aquifolium* has bright green leaves, which turn reddish in winter as the dense flower clusters appear, followed by blue-black berries. *M. × media* (including forms such as *M. × m.* 'Charity' and 'Winter Sun') is upright and taller, with longer racemes of flowers.

Schizostylis coccinea
KAFFIR LILY
Iridaceae

H 24in (60cm) **S** 12in (30cm)

Flowering from late summer to early winter, these evergreen rhizomatous perennials are grown for their tall spikes of gladiolus-like, cup-shaped flowers in shades of red, pink, magenta, and white. They are excellent in containers and as cut flowers. Later-flowering forms include *S.c.* var. *alba* (white flowers), *S.c.* 'Major' (large red flowers), and *S.c.* 'Sunrise' (large, salmon-pink flowers).

Skimmia japonica
Rutaceae

H and **S** 39in (1m)

A compact shrub with oval-shaped, slightly aromatic leaves, preferring partial shade. *S.j.* 'Rubella' is a male clone with red edges to the leaves, and panicles of dark-red flower buds which form in fall and winter and open in late winter and early spring. A female clone, such as *S.j.* 'Rogersii,' planted nearby, will form clusters of red berries which last until the next flush of flowers.

Viola × wittrockiana
PANSY
Violaceae

H 6 – 9in (15 – 23cm)
S 9 – 12in (23 – 30cm)

Hardy new pansy varieties mean that there are some in flower throughout the year, for winter containers and baskets as well as summer ones. *V. × wittrockiana* cultivars include many of the large-flowered, brightly colored pansies bred to flower during winter. They tolerate sun and shade, but need deadheading to maintain flowering. Flower colors include purple, blue, white, yellow, orange, pink, and red, as single or bicolored, often with central markings of a different color, including black.

Cyclamen hederifolium

Daphne bholua 'Gurkha'

Iris unguicularis

WATER & DAMP

Many patio gardens are large enough to include a tiny pond, and a simple one can be created quite easily from a container (see page 102). Having a small water feature allows you to grow a wider range of plants, and adds interest to the plant scheme as a consequence. Not all plants enjoy wet conditions; many are happier in swamp-like soil, which can be created next to a water feature by sinking a plastic liner, pierced to make it permeable, a spade's depth or so beneath the soil's surface.

Caltha palustris 'Flore Pleno'

Ligularia dentata 'Desdemona'

Aponogeton distachyos
WATER HAWTHORN
Aponogetonaceae
H 4 – 6in (10 – 15cm)
S 4ft (1.2m)

A frost-hardy aquatic perennial with bright green, long, oval leaves which float on the water surface from a submerged rhizome. Clusters of small, white, hawthorn-scented flowers are carried just above the water in spring and fall. Grow in soil or planting baskets in water about 3ft (1m) deep, preferably in full sun. Remove dead flowers and foliage from the water.

Caltha palustris
MARSH MARIGOLD
Ranunculaceae
H 4 – 16in (10 – 40cm)
S 18in (45cm)

A marginal perennial with dark green, kidney-shaped leaves and cup-shaped yellow or white flowers in spring and an occasional second flush in summer. Grow in very moist soil or a partially submerged planting basket, preferably in full sun. *C.p.* var. *alba* is compact with yellow-centered white flowers in early spring. *C.p.* 'Flore Pleno' has double yellow flowers.

Iris
WATER IRIS
Iridaceae
H 32in (80cm)

Hardy perennials with purple, blue, pink, red, yellow, or white flowers which enjoy slightly acidic marginal conditions in wet or very moist soil. *I. kaempferi* (*I. ensata*) has red-

purple flowers, the form 'Blue Peter' has bright blue flowers, and 'Moonlight Waves' has white flowers with green centers. *I. laevigata* has purple-blue flowers, the form 'Rosea' has pink flowers, and 'Variegata' has green- and white-striped foliage. (See pages 131 and 134, SEASONAL COLOR: SPRING and AUTUMN & WINTER).

Lagarosiphon major (formerly Elodea crispa)
CURLY WATER THYME
Hydrocharitaceae
H up to 3ft (1m) **S** indefinite

A submerged, hardy aquatic perennial with stems up to 3ft (1m) long, branching, and covered with curved, dark green leaves. Acts as an oxygenator, gradually forming a dense mass which will need reducing – not difficult, as the stems are easily broken. Remove all debris from the water. Tiny greenish-pink flowers appear among the leaves in summer.

Ligularia dentata
Compositae
H 3 – 5ft (1 – 1.5m) **S** 3ft (1m)

A hardy perennial which needs a constantly moist (but not wet) soil and full sun, and benefits from some shelter. It has rounded leaves with red-tinted lower leafstalks, and upright spikes of daisylike flowers in yellow or orange with brown centers, produced during summer and fall. *L.d.* 'Desdemona' has brownish leaves, purple beneath, and deep orange flowers.

Nymphaea
WATER LILY (miniature)
Nymphaeaceae
S 30 – 36in (75 – 90cm)

Herbaceous perennials with round, floating leaves and showy, sometimes scented, flowers in shades of red, pink, white, yellow, and blue. Choose small varieties, and grow in full sun. *N.* 'Albida' has red-tinted leaves and white flowers. *N.* 'Ellisiana' has dark green leaves and red flowers with orange stamens. The flowers of *N.* 'Indiana' are apricot, turning to dark orange-red, with orange stamens.

Pontederia cordata
PICKEREL WEED
Pontederiaceae
H 3 – 4ft (90 – 120cm)
S 24 – 30in (60 – 75cm)

A fully hardy marginal perennial which prefers to grow in full sun, and in no more than 4in (10cm) of water. Bright green, lance-shaped foliage may rise above, lie on, or remain below the surface of the water. Upright spikes of tubular, two-lipped, blue flowers are produced in late summer. *P.c.* var. *lancefolia* is taller, and has longer, narrower leaves.

Primula denticulata
DRUMSTICK PRIMULA
Primulaceae
H and **S** 18in (45cm)

A hardy, rosette-forming, deciduous perennial with long, rounded, mid-green leaves, whitish beneath. Prefers a neutral to acid soil that is

Pontederia cordata

constantly moist (but not wet), in full sun or partial shade. Robust, upright stems carry spherical clusters of tightly packed trumpet-shaped flowers of purple with a yellow center from spring to summer. *P. d. alba* has white flowers, and those of the variety 'Rubra' are reddish-purple.

Rodgersia pinnata
Saxifragaceae
H 4ft (1.2m) **S** 30in (75cm)

A clump-forming, rhizomatous perennial, which prefers to grow in a constantly moist soil, in full sun or partial shade, sheltered from cold winds. Leaves are divided, on long reddish-green stems, and so heavily veined that they appear crinkled. Loose spikes of small, star-shaped flowers are produced in summer, in shades of creamy-white, pink, or red. *R.p.* 'Superba' has bronze-purple young leaves and bright pink flowers.

HERBS & EDIBLE PLANTS

Lavandula angustifolia

Most gardeners, with only a tiny area in which to garden, long for a few plants that can be plucked and eaten fresh. Herbs are the ideal candidates for sunny situations, such as windowsills, and many of them can be grown very successfully from seed in small containers. With just a little more space, you could create a tiny herb garden, neatly edged in clipped boxwood, each section filled with a favorite herb.

You can grow herbs for their medicinal properties or their culinary value, or simply because you like the look of them. Their gentle colors and frequently aromatic scent have a wonderfully soothing effect, and many, like lavender or oregano, for example, attract bees or butterflies.

A few edible plants, notably lettuces, tomatoes, strawberries, beans, and potatoes, do well in containers, whether plastic growing bags, disguised with a simple wooden surround, or more elaborate specially constructed planters (terracotta pots for potatoes and strawberries have planting holes incorporated up the sides of the pot). Edible plants, to survive, need a rich soil and plenty of water, as well as sunshine to ripen the crops in the case of strawberries and tomatoes. Tomatoes, in particular, need sun, copious watering, and plenty of fertilizer if they are to produce worthwhile crops. They will need supporting on canes. Runner beans need similar fertilizing and watering. They can be staked on a cane wigwam (see pages 18-9), looking highly ornamental as well as offering a good crop of beans throughout the late summer months. Lettuces grow very easily from seed, and the oak-leaved forms are attractive enough to be used as edging to a small bed.

HERBS

Allium schoenoprasum
CHIVES
Alliaceae

H 12 – 24in (30 – 60cm)
S 4 – 6in (10 – 15cm)

A hardy, bulbous, clump-forming perennial grown for its edible, hollow, dark green leaves, which have a mild onion flavor. Grow in well-drained soil, preferably in full sun. Dense, round heads of purple (or occasionally white) flowers appear in summer. The flowers of *A.s.* 'Forescate' are deep pink.

Anthriscus cerefolium
CHERVIL
Umbelliferae

H 20 – 24in (50 – 60cm)
S 12in (30cm)

A hardy, upright annual with finely divided, aniseed-flavored leaves. Grows in full sun or partial shade in any well-drained soil, but watering must be maintained during drought, or it will bolt. Produces umbels of tiny white flowers in summer.

Lavandula angustifolia 'Hidcote'
LAVENDER
Labiatae

H 24in (60cm) **S** 30in (75cm)

A compact, hardy shrub, which likes full sun and a well-drained soil, but looks good in a container, at the front of a border, or as a low-growing hedge. It has silvery leaves and fragrant, dark purple flowers during summer, which may be picked and dried for use indoors in pot pourri or among clothes to deter moths.

Mentha
MINT
Labiatae

H 4 – 36in (10 – 90cm)
S 20in (50cm) – indefinite

Hardy, rhizomatous perennials, which will spread indefinitely if the roots are not restricted. Grow in any moist soil, in full sun, but restrict by planting in containers, or pots plunged into the soil. Forms include: M. × *gracilis* 'Variegata' (ginger mint); M. × *piperita citrata* (eau-de-Cologne mint); M. *pulegium* (pennyroyal); M. *requienii* (Corsican mint); M. *spicata* (spearmint); M. *suaveolens* (apple mint); and M. × *villosa alopecuroides* (Bowles' mint).

Ocimum basilicum
BASIL
Labiatae

H 12 – 24in (30 – 60cm)
S 12in (30cm)

Usually grown as a half-hardy annual, basil will need a warm,

Lavandula angustifolia 'Hidcote'   *Mentha* × *piperita*

sheltered position and a constant supply of water, in a well-drained soil mix. The bright green, pointed, oval leaves are delicious when cooked with tomato dishes. Spikes of pinkish, two-lipped flowers are produced in summer. *O.b.* 'Dark Opal' has dark red-purple leaves, and *O.b. minimum* is more compact.

Origanum vulgare
MARJORAM, OREGANO
Labiatae
H and S 12 – 24in (30 – 60cm)

A woody, bush-forming perennial with aromatic oval leaves, which are often used as flavorings for meat and soups. Enjoys growing in full sun, in a well-drained and preferably alkaline soil. Loose heads of small flowers are produced during summer, from pale to dark pink, or white. The form 'Aureum' has golden-yellow foliage, 'Compactum' is smaller and dome-shaped, and 'Variegatum' has yellow tips to the leaves.

Petroselinum crispum
PARSLEY
Umbelliferae
H 24 – 32in (60 – 80cm)
S 24in (60cm)

A hardy biennial more often grown as an annual, with bright green, edible foliage used in cooking or as a garnish. Grow in well-drained soil in full sun or partial shade. Forms include

Salvia officinalis 'Purpurascens'

P.c. 'Afro' (upright, with tightly curled leaves); 'Clivi' (compact); *neapolitanum* (Italian parsley, which has flatter leaves and a stronger flavor); and var. *tuberosum* (Hamburg parsley, which has edible roots).

Rosmarinus officinalis
ROSEMARY
Labiatae
H and S 3 – 5ft (1 – 1.5m)

A hardy, evergreen shrub with aromatic foliage and small two-lipped flowers in blue, purple, or white from late spring through to fall. Grow in full sun in a well-drained soil mix, individually or as a hedge. Forms include: 'Aureus' (yellow variegated leaves); 'Miss Jessop's Upright' (erect-growing, but vigorous with blue flowers); 'Prostratus' (low, trailing stems, but not so hardy); and 'Roseus' (pink flowers).

Salvia officinalis
SAGE
Labiatae
H 24 – 32in (60 – 80cm)
S 24 – 36in (60 – 90cm)

A woody, evergreen perennial with long, oval, aromatic leaves, used in such dishes as stuffings and sausages. Small, purple-blue flowers are produced in summer. Prefers moist, but well-drained soil in full sun or light shade, and will thrive in a container. Forms include: 'Icterina' (variegated yellow and green leaves); 'Purpurascens' (reddish-purple leaves); and 'Tricolor' (creamy white variegations on gray-green leaves, with young foliage also flushed pink).

EDIBLE PLANTS

Fragaria vesca
STRAWBERRY
Rosaceae
H 4 – 6in (10 – 15cm)
S indefinite

Ideal plants for growing in containers because their habit of spreading by runners means that they can get out of control in the garden. Grow in full sun or very light shade in moist, but

Lycopersicon esculentum 'Phyra'

well-drained soil. White flowers appear from early summer until fall, depending on variety, followed by the sweet red fruits. Cut runners off as they appear or root new plants by potting into containers of soil.

Lactuca sativa
LETTUCE
Compositae
H 10in (25cm)
S up to 12in (30cm)

The three main types – cabbage, leaf, and romaine– can all be grown in containers or soil, as long as they are well-fed and given enough water. They prefer full sun. Exotic leaf varieties, such as 'Lollo Blonda' and 'Lollo Rossa' do not form a heart as such, so leaves can be removed on a cut-and-come-again basis. The small, more compact, varieties of romaine lettuce are ideal for the smaller garden.

Lycopersicon esculentum
TOMATO
Solanaceae
H up to 4ft (1.2m)
S up to 24in (60cm)

Tomatoes may be grown in the ground, in growing bags, or in containers, under cover or outdoors (depending on the variety). Outdoors, the crop will depend on the weather, but varieties such as *L.e.* 'Gardener's Delight' or 'Phyra' are usually reliable choices. 'Tumbler' and

'Tiny Tim' are ideal for plant pots, windowboxes, and hanging baskets.

Phaseolus
RUNNER BEAN, STRING BEAN
Leguminosae
H up to 4ft (1.2m)
S 24in (60cm)

Dwarf varieties of green beans are suitable for growing in small gardens, either in the ground or in containers. Sow in late spring and grow in a sunny position, staking the plants if necessary. Dwarf runner bean varieties include 'Hammond's Dwarf Scarlet' and 'Pickwick'. Dwarf string beans include such varieties as 'Annabel,' 'Forum,' 'Masai,' and 'Vibel'.

Solanum tuberosum
POTATO
Solanaceae
H and S 24 – 36in (60 – 90cm)

Potatoes will grow in any container that is at least 12in (30cm) wide and deep with drainage holes in the base, and standing in a sunny position. Lay 2–3 sliced potatoes with at least one eye each on 4 – 5in (10 – 12cm) of compost or soil in the container and cover with a similar depth of compost or soil. Cover with another similar depth once the shoots are about 6in (15cm) tall, leaving the tips showing. Repeat until the shoots are within 2in (5cm) of the rim.

PLANT LISTS

A selection of plants (the majority of which are detailed in the Plant Finder on pages 120–137) for particular purposes or situations is given on these pages. The listing includes not only the best container and hanging basket plants, but also a few small trees and evergreen shrubs to give structure to the planting. Each plant is categorized according to type – tree, shrub, perennial, et cetera. There is a selection of plants for flower color and foliage color.

KEY
a = annual and biennial
a/p = tender perennials treated
   as annuals
b = bulb
c = climber
p = perennial
s = shrub
t = tree

Container plants

Agapanthus (p – blue)
Ageratum (a – blue)
Alonsoa (a – orange)
Argyranthemum (a/p – white, pink, yellow)
Begonia semperflorens (a – mixed colors)
Begonia x tuberhybrida (a/p – pink, red, orange, white)
Bidens ferulifolia (a – yellow)
Brachyscome iberidifolia (a – blue)
Buxus sempervirens (s – foliage)
Cordyline australis (p – foliage)
Diascia (p – pink, orange)
Felicia amelloides (a – blue)
Fuchsia (s – pink, purple, red)
Helichrysum petiolare (a/p – foliage)
Hosta (p – foliage)
Hyacinthus (b – mixed colors)
Hydrangea (s – blue, pink, white)
Impatiens walleriana (a/p – white, pink, red)
Laurus nobilis (s – foliage)
Lobelia (a – blue, pink, white)
Narcissus (b – yellow, white)
Nemisia (a – mixed colors)
Pelargonium (a/p – orange, pink, red, white)
Petunia (a/p – mixed colors)
Phormium (p – foliage)
Primula (p – mixed colors)
Senecio cineraria (a/p – foliage)
Tagetes (a – yellow, orange)
Tropaeolum (a – red, orange, yellow)
Tulipa (b – mixed colors)
Verbena x hybrida (a/p – mixed colors)
Viola x wittrockiana (a – mixed colors)

Hanging basket plants

Ageratum (a – blue)
Alonsoa (a – orange)
Argyranthemum (a/p – white, pink, yellow)
Begonia semperflorens (a – mixed colors)
Begonia x tuberhybrida (a/p – pink, red, orange, white)
Bidens ferulifolia (a – yellow)
Brachyscome iberidifolia (a – blue)
Diascia (p – pink, orange)
Felicia amelloides (a – blue)
Fuchsia (s – pink, purple, red)
Glechoma hederacea 'Variegata' (a – foliage)
Hedera helix (p – foliage)
Helichrysum petiolare (a/p – foliage)
Impatiens walleriana (a – white, pink, red)
Lobelia erinus (a – blue, pink, white)
Lotus berthelottii (p – orange, foliage)
Narcissus (b – yellow, white)
Pelargonium (a/p – orange, pink, red, white)
Petunia (a/p – mixed colors)
Plectranthus coleoides (a/p – foliage)
Primula (p – mixed colors)
Scaevola (a/p – purple, blue)
Senecio cinerea (a/p – foliage)
Tagetes (a – yellow, orange)
Tropaeolum (a – red, orange, yellow)
Tulipa (b – mixed colors)
Verbena x hybrida (a/p – mixed colors)
Viola x wittrockiana (a – mixed colors)

Plants for color

Blue/mauve flowers
Agapanthus spp. and cvs. (p)
Ageratum spp. and cvs. (a)
Ajuga reptans (p)
Aquilegia flabellata (p)
Aster amellus (p)
Brunnera macrophylla (p)
Campanula spp. and cvs. (p)
Caryopteris x clandonensis (s)
Catananche caerulea (p)
Ceanothus spp. and cvs. (s)
Clematis cvs. (c)
Delphinium spp. and cvs. (p)
Echinops ritro (p)
Gentiana spp. and cvs. (p)
Geranium spp. and cvs. (p)
Hebe spp. and cvs. (s)
Hosta spp. and cvs. (p)
Hyacinthoides hispanica (b)
Hydrangea spp. and cvs. (s)
Iris spp. and cvs. (p)
Lavandula angustifolia (s)
Meconopsis spp. (p)
Muscari spp. and cvs. (b)
Nepeta spp. and cvs. (p)
Nigella damascena (a)
Omphalodes cappadocica (p)
Penstemon heterophyllus (p)
Perovskia atriplicifolia (s)
Plumbago spp. (s)
Polemonium caeruleum (p)
Primula spp. and cvs. (p)
Pulmonaria spp. and cvs. (p)
Salvia spp. and cvs. (p & s)
Scabiosa caucasica (p)
Veronica spp. and cvs. (p)
Viola spp. and cvs. (p & a)

Yellow, gold and orange flowers
Achillea spp. and cvs. (p)
Anthemis tinctoria (p)
Aurinia saxatilis (p)
Buphthalmum salicifolium (p)
Clematis tangutica (p)
Coreopsis verticillata (p)
Coronilla valentina (s)
Crocus cvs. (b)
Cytisus x praecox cvs. (s)
Digitalis lutea (p)
Euphorbia spp. and cvs. (p)
Geum 'Lady Strathenden' (p)
Helenium spp. and cvs. (p)
Heliopsis spp. and cvs. (p)
Hemerocallis spp. and cvs. (p)
Inula spp. and cvs. (p)
Jasminum nudiflorum (s)
Limnanthes douglasii (a)
Lysimachia nummularia 'Aurea' (p)
Mahonia aquifolium (s)
Narcissus cvs. (b)
Paeonia mlokosewitschii (p)

Primula spp. and cvs. (p)
Rosa cvs. (s & c)
Rudbeckia spp. and cvs. (a & p)
Solidago spp. and cvs. (p)
Tagetes cvs. (a)
Trollius spp. and cvs. (p)
Tropaeolum majus (a)
Tulipa cvs. (b)
Verbascum spp. and cvs. (p)
Viola x wittrockiana (a)

Red flowers
Achillea 'Cerise Queen' (p)
Alcea rosea (p)
Astilbe 'Fanal' (p)
Centranthus ruber (p)
Cosmos atrosanguineus (p)
Dianthus 'Brympton Red' (p)
Fuchsia cvs. (s)
Geum 'Mrs Bradshaw' (p)
Impatiens cvs. (a)
Lobelia 'Cherry Ripe' (p)
Lupinus 'Inverewe Red' (p)
Lychnis chalcedonica (p)
Paeonia spp. and cvs.
Papaver orientale (p)
Pelargonium cvs. (a)
Penstemon 'Cherry Ripe' (p)
Petunia cvs. (a)
Potentilla 'Gibson's Scarlet' (p)
Potentilla 'Red Ace' (s)
Rosa cvs. (c &s)
Tulipa cvs. (b)

Pink flowers
Anemone x hybrida (p)
Antirrhinum cvs. (a)
Armeria spp. and cvs. (p)
Aster spp. and cvs. (p)
Cistus spp. and cvs. (s)
Colchicum spp. (b)
Cyclamen hederifolium (b)
Dahlia cvs. (b)
Deutzia spp. and cvs. (s)
Dianthus spp. and cvs. (p)
Diascia spp. and cvs. (p)
Dicentra spp. and cvs. (p)
Erigeron 'Charity' (p)
Fuchsia cvs. (s)
Geranium spp. and cvs. (p)
Hydrangea spp. and cvs. (s)
Impatiens cvs. (a)
Lamium roseum (p)

Lychnis flos-jovis (p)
Malva moschata (p)
Papaver orientale 'Cedric Morris' (p)
Penstemon 'Hidcote Pink' (p)
Persicaria spp. and cvs. (p)
Petunia cvs. (a)
Primula spp. and cvs. (p)
Sedum spectabile (p)
Sidalcea spp. and cvs. (p)
Tulipa cvs. (b)

Purple flowers

Aster spp. and cvs. (p)
Centaurea spp. and cvs. (p)
Erigeron 'Dunkelste Aller' (p)
Erysimum 'Bowles Mauve' (p)
Exacum affine (a)
Geranium spp. and cvs. (p)
Hebe spp. and cvs. (s)
Hyacinthus cvs. (b)
Liatris spicata (p)
Linaria purpurea (p)
Lythrum spp. and cvs. (p)
Osteospermum jucundum (p)
Penstemon 'Burgundy' (p)
Petunia cvs. (a)
Salvia hormium (a)
Stachys macrantha (p)
Syringa cvs. (s)
Verbena bonariensis (p)

White flowers

Achillea ptarmica 'The Pearl' (p)
Anemone x *hybrida* 'Honorine Jobert' (p)
Anthemis punctata cupaniana (p)
Argyranthemum frutescens (a/p)
Astilbe 'Irrlicht' (p)
Campanula latiloba alba (p)
Cistus spp. (s)
Convolvulus cneorum (s)
Dianthus 'Haytor White' (p)
Echinops sphaerocephalus (p)
Geranium sanguineum 'Album' (p)
Gypsophila paniculata 'Bristol Fairy' (p)
Iberis amara (a)
Lamium maculatum 'White Nancy' (p)
Leucanthemum 'Everest' (p)
Nicotiana cvs. (a)
Olearia spp. (s)
Osmanthus spp. and cvs. (s)
Osteospermum 'Whirligig' (a/p)
Petunia cvs. (a)
Polygonatum x *hybridum* (p)
Potentilla 'Abbotswood' (s)
Prunus spp. and cvs. (s & t)
Pulmonaria 'Sissinghurst White' (p)
Spiraea 'Bridal Wreath' (s)
Viburnum spp. and cvs. (s)
Yucca spp. (s)

Foliage color

Silver foliage

Artemisia spp. and cvs. (p)
Cerastium tomentosum (p)
Convolvulus cneorum (s)
Cynara cardunculus (p)
Elaeagnus 'Quicksilver' (s)
Eryngium giganteum (p)
Hebe pinguifolia 'Pagei' (s)
Lavandula angustifolia (s)
Melianthus major (a/p)
Onopordum spp. (a)
Pyrus salicifolia 'Pendula' (t)
Santolina chamaecyparis (p)
Senecio cineraria (a/p)
Stachys byzantina (p)
Tanacetum haradjanii (p)

Purple foliage

Acer palmatum 'Atropurpureum' (t)
Ajuga reptans 'Atropurpurea' (p)
Berberis thunbergii 'Atropurpurea' (s)
Clematis recta 'Purpurea' (p)
Cordyline australis 'Atropurpurea' (p)
Corylus maxima 'Purpurea' (s)
Cotinus coggygria 'Royal Purple' (s)
Dahlia 'Bishop of Llandaff' (p)
Foeniculum vulgare 'Purpureum' (p)
Heuchera micrantha 'Palace Purple' (p)
Lobelia cardinalis (p)
Phormium tenax 'Purpureum' (p)
Prunus cerasifera 'Nigra' (t)
Ricinus communis 'Gibsonii' (a)
Rosa glauca (s)
Salvia officinalis 'Purpurascens' (s)
Sedum maximum atropurpureum (p)
Viola riviniana Purpurea Group (p)
Vitis vinifera 'Purpurea' (c)

Golden foliage

Acer japonicum 'Aurea' (t)
Carex stricta 'Bowles' Golden' (p)
Filipendula ulmaria 'Aurea' (p)
Fuchsia 'Golden Treasure' (s)
Gleditsia triacanthos 'Sunburst' (t)
Hebe armstrongii (s)
Hedera helix 'Buttercup' (c)
Hosta spp. and cvs. (p)
Humulus lupulus 'Aureus' (c)
Ligustrum ovalifolium 'Aureum' (s)
Lonicera nitida 'Baggesen's Gold' (s)
Lysimachia nummularia 'Aurea' (p)
Milium effusum 'Aureum' (p)
Oreganum vulgare 'Aureum' (p)

Philadelphus coronarius 'Aureus' (s)
Physocarpus opulifolius 'Luteus' (s)
Robinia pseudoacacia 'Frisia' (t)
Sambucus racemosa 'Plumosa Aurea' (s)
Tanecetum parthenium 'Aureum' (p)
Taxus baccata 'Aurea' (t)

Blue foliage

Elymus magellanicus (p)
Eucalyptus gunnii (t)
Hosta 'Blue Boy' (p)
Hosta 'Hadspen Blue' (p)
Hosta 'Halcyon' (p)
Hosta sieboldiana 'Elegans' (p)

Variegated foliage

Acer negundo 'Variegatum' (t)
Aktinidia kolomikta (s)
Aquilegia vulgaris 'Woodside' (p)
Aralia elata 'Aureovariegata' (t)
Astrantia major 'Sunningdale Variegated' (p)
Brunnera macrophylla 'Hadspen Cream' (p)
Cornus alba 'Elegantissima' (s)
Cortaderia selloana 'Gold Band' (p)
Elaeagnus pungens 'Maculata' (s)
Eryngium bourgatii (p)
Euonymus fortunei 'Emerald 'n' Gold' (s)
Euphorbia marginata (a)
Fragaria x *ananassa* 'Variegata' (p)
Hakonechloa macra 'Aureola' (p)
Hedera spp. and cvs. (c)
Hosta spp. and cvs. (p)
Ilex spp. and cvs. (t)
Iris pallida 'Variegata' (p)
Lamium maculatum (p)
Lonicera japonica 'Aureo-reticulata' (c)
Miscanthus sinensis 'Zebrinus' (p)
Phalaris arundinacea 'Picta' (p)
Phormium tenax 'Sundowner' (p)
Pleioblastus auricomus (p)
Pulmonaria saccharata (p)
Rhamnus alaternus 'Argenteovariegata' (t)
Salvia officinalis 'Icterina' (s)
Silybum marianum (a)
Sisyrinchium striatum 'Aunt May' (p)
Symphytum x *uplandicum* 'Variegatum' (p)
Tanecetum vulgare 'Silver Lace' (p)
Vinca major 'Variegata' (s)

Small trees

Acer japonicum
Betula pendula 'Youngii'
Cercis siliquastrum
Ilex x *altaclarensis*
Laburnum x *waterei* 'Vossii'
Malus 'Profusion'
Prunus serrula
Pyrus salicifolia 'Pendula'
Sorbus hupehensis

Evergreen shrubs

Abelia spp. and cvs.
Azara spp.
Berberis spp. and cvs.
Buxus sempervirens
Ceanothus ssp. and cvs.
Choisya ternata
Convolvulus cneorum
Cotoneaster spp. and cvs.
Daphne spp. and cvs.
Elaeagnus pungens
Escalonia spp. and cvs.
Euonymus fortunei
Garrya elliptica
Hebe spp. and cvs.
Ilex spp. and cvs.
Laurus nobilis
Mahonia spp. and cvs.
Osmanthus spp. and cvs.
Photinia spp. and cvs.
Pieris spp. and cvs.
Prunus lusitanicus
Rhododendron spp. and cvs.
Sarcococca spp. and cvs.
Skimmia japonica
Viburnum tinus
Vinca spp. and cvs.

GLOSSARY

A

Annual Plant that completes its cycle of germination from setting seed through to dying in a single growing season.

B

Biennial Plant requiring two growing seasons to flower and seed.
Bract Leaf at base of flower stalk or flower head; may resemble a small, normal leaf or, in some plants, be large and brightly colored.
Bulb Plant storage organ, usually formed underground, containing the following year's growth buds.
Bulbil A very small or secondary bulb that forms, e.g. on lilies.

C

Calyx Usually green, outer part of a flower, formed from the sepals, that encases the petals in bud.
Classification Botanically and for ease of identification, plants are grouped according to family, genus, species, and variety or cultivar. For example, with the rose family, *Rosaceae*, *Rosa* = genus, *R. gallica* = species, *R.g. var. officinalis* = variety, and *R.g.* 'Versicolor' = hybrid or cultivar.
Climber Plant that uses other plants or objects to grow upwards. Without support, their (usually) lax stems will creep along the ground.
Corm A swollen stem base that acts as a storage organ, similar to a bulb, but of a single piece without layers; it is annual, with the following year's corm developing from a bud close to the original.
Crown The part of a herbaceous plant from where new stems are produced and to where they die back in fall.
Cultivar A man-made or cultivated variety, produced by hybridization. It will usually have a name chosen by the breeder, e.g. *Clematis* 'Bill Mackenzie'.
Cutting A section of a plant removed for propagation. Cuttings may be root, basal (new growth taken from a herbaceous plant in spring), greenwood (taken from the tip of young growth), softwood (young growth taken at the start of the growing season), semi-ripe (half-ripened stem taken during the growing season), or hardwood (mature stem taken at the end of the growing season).

D

Deciduous Plant losing its leaves annually; semi-deciduous plants lose some of their leaves.
Division Splitting of a plant clump into parts containing roots and shoots; normally done when the plant is dormant, for propagation.
Double flowers Applied to a flower head or bloom having more petals than the original species, e.g. *Bellis perennis* 'Alba Plena', a double version of the common daisy.

E

Evergreen Plant retaining its leaves at the end of the growing season, though older leaves may be lost through the year.

F

Family See classification.
Flower head Mass of small flowers that appear as one flower.

G

Gazebo Ornamental garden structure, usually of wood or iron, used as a raised viewing platform.
Genus see Classification
Glaucous Covered in a bluish-gray, bluish-green, or bluish-white bloom.

H

Half-hardy Plant that withstands low temperatures but not freezing.
Harden off Allowing greenhouse-raised plants gradually to acclimatize to outside conditions by leaving them out for increasing periods before planting out.
Hardy Plant that tolerates year-round conditions in temperate climates, including normal frost, without protection.
Herbaceous Non-woody plant that dies down to its rootstock in winter.
Humus Largely decomposed organic matter naturally present in or introduced into the top layer of soil; improves soil fertility and water-holding capacity.
Hybrid A plant resulting from crossing two different species, often of the same genus, usually by cultivation, but sometimes occurring in the wild. An F1 hybrid is a plant that is propagated using the seed from two true parent plants, after hand-pollinating. Plants raised from hybrid seed (including F1 hybrids) often do not breed true to type.

I

Inflorescence A group or arrangement of flowers on a stem, such as panicles and racemes.
Intercrop A fast-growing crop grown between rows of a later and slower crop, e.g. lettuces between onions.

K

Knot garden Ornamental ground pattern of low hedging, infilled with planting or hard materials; intricate interweaving of the linear planting was a favorite device of Tudor and Elizabethan gardens.

M

Marginal Plant that grows partially submerged in shallow water or moist soil at a pond edge.
Microclimate Normally refers to small area protected from extreme weather and so experiencing different climatic conditions from its locality. Microclimates can be created, for example, by walls.
Mulch Layer of organic or inorganic material added to the surface of the soil to retain moisture, help suppress weeds and gradually improve fertility.

O

Offset Plant that is reproduced naturally from the base of the parent plant.

P

Panicle A flower stem (inflorescence) that branches into several small stems or stalks, with the youngest flowers at the top, e.g. lilac.
Perennial A plant that lives for longer than two seasons.
Picotee A *dianthus* (pink) having light petals edged with a darker color.

R

Raceme A long, unbranched flower stem (inflorescence), the flowers opening in sequence from the bottom upwards.
Rhizome An underground, often creeping, stem acting as a storage organ, from which roots and shoots grow.
Rootball The roots together with the soil adhering to them when a plant is lifted, e.g. for transplanting.

S

Sepals Green outer parts of a flower, collectively forming the calyx.
Single flowers Applied to a flower that has the normal number of petals for its species, such as a daisy.
Species See classification.
Standard A tree or shrub with a length of bare stem below the first branches; some shrubs, e.g. roses and fuschias, can be trained to form standards.

T

Topiary The art of clipping evergreen shrubs into specific shapes – such as cubes, pyramids, or spheres.
Type Used to refer to an original plant species.

V

Variety A variant of a plant species, arising either naturally or as a result of selection.

INDEX

ACKNOWLEDGMENTS

**The photographer, publishers and authors would like to thank the following
people and organizations who kindly allowed us to photograph their gardens:**
Don Brant; Tom & Jo Frosdick and their neighbors; Leeann MacKenzie; Jan Scruton.

**The authors and publishers are also grateful to the following for
their help and support in the production of this book:**
Val Bradley for the text for the Plant Finder; Lisa Dyer, Lisa Pendreigh and Sorcha Hitchcox for
editorial help; Dr Peter Boyce, Tony Lord and Brian Matthew for help with plant
checking and identification.

Picture credits:
All photographs Collins & Brown copyright except the following:
(T = top; B= bottom; R = right; L = left; C= centre; M = middle)

Garden Picture Library: p. 6 (John Glover); p. 12 (John Glover); p. 26 (Juliet Wade); p. 27
(BR - Marie O'Hara); p. 61 (TR - Robert Estall) & (B - Juliet Wade); p. 74 (CL - Lamontagne);
p. 82 (Lynne Brotchie); p. 84 (Marie O'Hara); p. 85 (Linda Burgess); p. 90 (BR - Lynne Brotchie);
p. 94 (Friedrich Strauss); p. 95 (TR - Friedrich Strauss & BR - Linda Burgess).

Michelle Garrett: p. 54 (BL); p. 68 (TR, BL); p. 69; p. 98 (TR); p. 122 (TL).

**Collins & Brown Limited would like to thank the following photographers
for taking the following photographs:**
Michelle Garrett: p. 14; p. 15; p. 16; p. 17; p. 18; p. 19; p. 20; p. 21; p. 22; p. 23; p. 28; p. 29; p. 32 (TL,
CR); p. 33; p. 34; p. 35 (TR); p. 36 (TL); p. 37 (TL, TR, BR); p. 38; p. 39; p. 40; p. 41; p. 42; p. 43; p.
44; p. 46 (BL); p. 47 (TL, BR); p. 48 (BR); p. 51; p. 52 (TR); p. 53 (TR); p 56 (BL); p. 57; p. 58; p. 62;
p. 63; p. 64; p. 65; p. 66; p. 67; p. 68 (TL); p. 70; p. 71 (TL, TR, BL); p. 72; p. 73; p. 74 (BL); p. 76; p.
77; p. 78; p. 79; p. 80 (TL, TM; BL); p. 81; p. 83; p. 86 (CM, CR, BM); p. 87; p. 88 (BL); p. 89; p. 90
(TR); p. 91; p. 96; p. 97; p. 99; p. 100; p. 101; p. 102; p. 103; p. 105; p. 106 (BL, BR); p. 107 (BL); p.
108 (TR, BL, BM); p. 109 (TM, TR, BL, BM); p. 110 (CR, BL, BM, BR); p. 111 (TR, BR); p. 112
(BR); p. 115 (BR); p .116 (BL); p. 117 (TL, TR, CR); p. 130 (TL); p. 136 (TL).

Howard Rice: p. 50 (BR); p. 114 (BR); p. 119; p. 121; p. 122 (BM, BR); p. 123 (CM, BM, BR); p. 125
(TL, TM, TR, CR); p. 126; p. 127 (TR, CR); p. 128 (TL, TR, CR); p. 129; p. 130 (BR); p. 131; p. 132;
p. 133 (T2ndL, T2ndR, CL); p. 134; p. 135; p. 136 (BM, BR); p. 137.

Steven Wooster: p. 1; p. 2; p. 7; p. 8; p. 9; p. 10; p. 11; p. 13; p. 24; p. 25; p. 27 (TL); p. 30; p. 31; p. 32
(BL); p. 35 (B); p. 36 (BR); p. 37 (BL); p. 45; p. 49; p. 50 (TR); p. 55; p. 56 (BR); p. 59; p. 60; p. 75; p.
88 (TL); p. 92; p. 93; p. 98 (BM); p. 118; p. 123 (CR, BL): p. 124; p. 127 (TL, TM, CM, BR); p. 128
(TM); p. 133 (TL, TR, CR).